BAFFERT

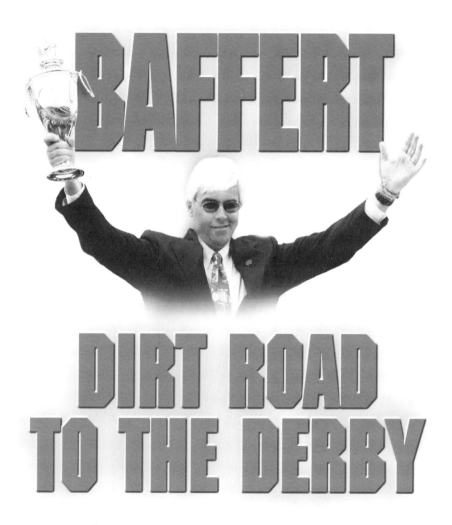

BAFFERT

DIRT ROAD TO THE DERBY

By Kentucky Derby winning trainer Bob Baffert with Steve Haskin

THE BLOOD-HORSE, INC. ■ LEXINGTON, KENTUCKY

ISBN 1-58150-025-4

Printed in Hong Kong
First Edition: November 1999
1 2 3 4 5 6 7 8 9 10

This book is dedicated to my father,

The Chief, who introduced me to horses

and racing at such a young age

and gave me the opportunity

to live out his dream.

CONTENTS

INTRODUCTION

s Bob Baffert's comet tears across the sky, no one can predict whether it will come crashing to Earth or continue to light up the heavens. All indications point to the latter.

For three months, I attempted to grab hold of that comet, but at times it proved to be as elusive as a moonbeam. One moment, my hand was aglow with the wit and wisdom that shines from Bob Baffert's mind, and the next, I held nothing but air.

Although I have known Bob since 1992, I am the first to admit I have as much in common with his world as I do the planet Pluto. To a Jewish kid growing up on the streets of Brooklyn, New York, the adventures and misadventures of someone from Nogales, Arizona, were something I could relate to only through Saturday morning TV serials. After all, Nogales, in my mind, was nothing more than a saloon, a livery stable, and a hitching post.

But then, the world of "Cowboy Bob" collided with mine. At the urging of his main client and close friend Mike Pegram, Bob ventured into the realm of the Thoroughbred, eventually bidding farewell to Quarter Horse racing, which had nurtured and sustained him since he was a teenager.

He brought to his new world a sense of humor that lied somewhere between Will Rogers and the cast of "Hee Haw." Unaccustomed to such fun and frivolity, the scribes moved in for the kill. But armed with nothing more than a notepad and a tape recorder, we were no match for the quick triggered tongue of this new gunslinger from Nogales.

The name Bob Baffert first came to my attention in the fall of 1992 while I was writing my weekly feature "Countdown to the Cup" for *Daily Racing Form*, in which I provided the latest news and results leading up to the Breeders' Cup. I had to call Bob occasionally because he had Thirty Slews pointing for the Breeders' Cup Sprint, and with two consecutive stakes victories under his belt, Thirty Slews was one of the contenders worth following closely. The voice on the other end of the phone meant little to me other than it belonged to one of those congenial young Southern California trainers whom I'd most likely never hear of again.

But I kept hearing the voice more often. Not because I'd keep calling him, but because he'd keep calling me. How refreshing to find a trainer so gregarious and helpful, I thought. Of course, I didn't know this was the guy who used to sell eggs for his father when he was a kid and had become so good at salesmanship, he could have sold a crate of eggs to someone on a cholesterol-free diet.

It seemed as if good ol' Bob would call me whenever Thirty Slews moved his bowels or to inform me of all the reasons why he should be higher on my Top Ten list. Although I appreciated the call and all his help, I didn't realize that every time I hung up, I had purchased a dozen eggs. It was like playing poker with one of my boyhood Western heroes, Brett Maverick. When Maverick turned on the charm, you never even noticed him pulling that fifth ace out of his boot. Even now, Bob can be holding five of a kind in his hand or peddling me whatever goods he has to sell that day, and I just learn to accept it.

The first inclination is to run him out of town on a rail, but there is such a personable and generous man underneath that devilish facade, you wind up backing off and enjoying the show. Talking to those close to him on the racetrack, you find out about all the people he has helped financially. One of his assistants said there isn't a softer touch on the backstretch. And this is a man who lost a million bucks in Triple Crown bonus money in 1997 and '98 by a total distance of a half-length, and afterward was just as amiable and accommodating as always.

But I knew it wouldn't be easy to tackle the project of chronicling Bob Baffert's life. How could I attempt to contain that restless spirit long enough for him to focus on all that has happened in his life? How could I take a mind that can be arid when preoccupied and turn it into the fertile garden where witty and profound thoughts spring to life with such ease?

When everything was flowing smoothly, I found myself not only writing about Bob Baffert's life, but living it. With each paragraph, my Saturday morning serials came to life, and I have to admit, it was hard changing the channel. I was taken to places I'd never been — the bush tracks of Arizona, shootouts, rodeos, and cattle drives. I saw both the beautiful and nefarious side of racing. And most of all, I learned about a man who, despite his human frailties, set his sights on greatness, and achieved it.

But no matter how high he climbed up the celebrity ladder, there was always a member of his family to keep the ladder sturdy. As supportive as they were, they would always be there to remind him that it takes only one slight slip to fall heavily to the ground. At a party given by Robert and Beverly Lewis following Silver Charm's failed attempt at a Triple Crown sweep, Bob got up and began to express his gratitude and remorse to the point of sounding maudlin. Just then, his brother Bill shouted across the room, "Loooser!" Jolted back to reality, Bob broke up laughing and quickly returned to being Bob.

I also learned how complex a simple person can be, and how simple a complex person can be. This wasn't Woody Stephens, in his twilight years, spinning yarns and recalling a long and storied career. This was a person whose career still is very much a work in progress. Perhaps, one day there will be a need for someone to pick up where we have left off. Bob's life is moving faster now than any of his Quarter Horses ever did. He overcame the label of sprinting trainer, and for the past three years has been basking in the limelight of the classics. Now all that's left for him to prove is that he has the stamina to go the distance.

Steve Haskin
Hamilton Square, New Jersey
June 1999

11

SO CLOSE WITH CAVONNIER

"I had never seen Bobby so disheartened. Cavonnier's loss haunted him for a year. Even when Silver Charm won the Del Mar Futurity, all he could think about was Cavonnier. That thing ate at him and ate at him. To get that close and get beat a nose, that was his one shot and he didn't get there. He never got it out of his system. In his mind, he was never going to get back there again. He'd watch the race over and over again and it just tore at him like nothing I've ever seen. When he went back with Silver Charm, he went to the Derby Museum to watch the slide presentation from the year before. When he walked out of there, he had tears in his eyes. He said to himself, "I've got to win this race." — Brad McKenzie

I had just won the 1996 Santa Anita Derby with Cavonnier. All those years training Quarter Horses; all those years training nothing but sprinters; and, just like that, here I am with a Derby horse. I was actually going to the Kentucky Derby. Man, I was flying high. I arrived at Churchill Downs before the horse, and was waiting for the press. I mean I am one press-hungry sonofagun. I was like a media whoremonger at the time. So I show up and there's one photographer from the Louisville *Courier-Journal* and some cute, little brown-haired girl from WAVE-TV. That's it.

I had been to Churchill Downs once before, in 1994, to run Arches of Gold on the Derby undercard for Mike Pegram, who was responsible for getting me started in Thoroughbreds. Mike owns a

12

number of McDonald's franchises in Washington state, and I don't even want to think where I'd be today if it wasn't for him. He's not only my biggest client, he's one of my closest friends. But there's a big difference coming to Churchill for an undercard race and coming with a Derby horse. You just don't feel it.

But when I came this time, I looked at those twin spires and I was like a kid walking into Toys R Us for the first time. I was overwhelmed. I worked Cavonnier a couple of times, but I really didn't get that much attention. I had won the Santa Anita Derby, but most people only knew me as Bob Baffert, former Quarter Horse trainer and trainer of sprinters. Cavonnier was a tough California-bred gelding who'll always hold a special place in my heart for getting me to my first Derby.

It wasn't until the pre-race favorite, Unbridled's Song, came into our barn that I started to get some attention. The horse had developed a foot problem, and each day, Churchill Downs would set up a podium on the other end of the barn for his trainer, Jim Ryerson, to address the press. Every morning, it was a mob scene over there, and I was just getting the residuals down at my end. It was like, "Hey, you guys want to talk to me? I'll tell you anything you want to know. I've got a lot to talk about." I had twenty years of training stored up in me, and there was lot of shit I'd been wanting to say for a long time. But in the Quarter Horse business, there's nobody to tell it to.

Little by little, I got to talking and joking, and did this television deal every day. Every afternoon, I actually would go back to the hotel and watch myself on TV to see how I did. And I have to admit, I sucked. When the camera came on, I was nervous, and I just wasn't being myself. When you first start doing something like this, you try so hard to sound intelligent, so you start thinking what you're going to say instead of just letting it come out naturally. As soon as that little light came on, I locked up.

But I learned how to relax, and I started getting better every day. I would resort to an old Quarter Horse expression that would begin every sentence. Before saying anything, we'd always begin with, "Ah tell you what." Everything wound up going really, really smooth the whole time I was there. The horse was training great, and I was just hoping to light the board. I would have been happy just to get a piece of it. Each morning after I got up, I'd watch the morning Derby show and find out who was working that day and what was going on with each horse. I'd watch it for an hour. The trainers would come on and tell how their horses were doing and what kind of strategy they were going to use. So, I was the only trainer who knew everyone's strategy, because I was the only one who was watching TV at that hour and not at the racetrack.

I really never got caught up in the history of the race and what I was a part of. I was just enjoying the moment and the media. What I did get caught up in was the whole Unbridled's Song deal. I found it very entertaining. What that horse had to go through, it proved he was a great horse. They never let Jim Ryerson train him, and it was total chaos. If he didn't have that foot problem, it would have been a totally different story. There was no doubt he was the best horse in the race. With all the problems he had Derby Week, he went and drew post nineteen. I remember seeing one of the reporters after the draw and telling him, "How can any horse stabled in my barn have such bad karma?"

I'll never forget the day of the race. I started really getting nervous the night before, because I knew I had a chance. I knew Cavonnier was going to run well, but there's always that doubt in your mind. I only hoped that when they hit the three-eighths pole, he didn't throw it in reverse. Derby morning, I was at the Executive West hotel, and I got a message from Chris McCarron to call him. I went to his room and we talked about the race. I told him, "Chris, all I can say is that he's training great. You've won this race, so you know what you've got to do and where you have to be." He told me, whoever is in front at the eighth pole will win the race. So I said, "Okay, then, I think you should put in a big run from the three-eighths pole to the eighth pole and stagger in, because they're all going to stagger in on their hands and knees. I don't think any of these horses want to go that far, so maybe we can get lucky."

Chris is a real smart rider, and he already had everything mapped out in his mind. He was going to be laying anywhere from three to five lengths off the pace, getting a good spot, and keeping him out of trouble. Earlier in the day, we ran Criollito for Bob and Beverly Lewis in the Churchill Downs Handicap, and he won. It was awesome. Even winning a race on the undercard in front of all those people was special. I mean, we were pumped. As soon as Criollito won, I started feeling really confident. If he's doing great, it means Cavonnier is doing great. Now it was just a matter of whether or not he was good enough.

We came back to the barn and we were feeling great. Poor Bob Lewis missed the race. He was at the airport at the time and watched it there. His daughter was about to give birth back in California, and he had to leave. As it turned out, his granddaughter, Chloe, was born on Derby Day. That birth was to have more significance than any of us could have imagined.

Finally, I'm in the barn office with my brothers Bill and P. A., and they tell us they want everyone in the Derby to bring their horses to the track and meet by the gap. Now I'm starting to get butterflies. Ryerson and Buzz Chace, who picked out Unbridled's

Song as a yearling for Ernie Paragallo, start getting their horse out, but I'm not ready to go. It was still early. I told Buzz, "Hey, they're not going to run this race without us. You got the favorite, buddy, and I got the third or fourth choice. You think they're going to run the race without us? I don't think so. Let's just cool it for a while." So they waited, and we went out together. I also had Semoran in the race, but I really didn't want to run him. He wasn't on the same level as these horses going a mile and a quarter.

We got out on the track, and the crowd was screaming. It was fantastic. We're walking four abreast — me, my brothers, and my veterinarian, Vince Baker. We were with Cavonnier, and Semoran was behind us. The crowd starts yelling for Cavonnier — "Go Cavonnier! Go get 'em Bob!" — and no one is yelling for Unbridled's Song. We were amazed. I realized these were my true fans, the ones behind the fences. I turned to my brothers, and I said, "Now I know how Wyatt Earp felt at the OK Corral." You just feel like you're going to battle. You're breathing hard, there are cameras everywhere, and you're so emotional. You can feel the excitement all around you.

We got to the paddock, and I put the saddle on both horses. Chris came out, and my only instructions to him were, "Go out there and make me famous." He said, "You got it."

I was really looking forward to hearing "My Old Kentucky Home." I told my wife, Sherry, "Wait until you hear it. It's an unbelievable moment." But that year, they got some Country Western singer to do it and it sounded like shit. Even Sherry said, "That was it?" We all get up to the box, and we're nervous. When they broke from the gate, it was like, "Oh my God." All you see is this full gate of horses charging out of there, and the roar from the crowd is deafening.

16

Cavonnier breaks clean, and I see him go by the stands and he's in a great spot going into the first turn. He gets around the turn in perfect position, and down the backstretch he's six or seven lengths off the pace and going beautifully.

Meanwhile, Unbridled's Song is out there cooking. They're going real fast up front. Usually, when I watch a race with Sherry, I'm telling her what's going on, because she doesn't go to the races that much. She keeps asking me, "What do you think?" and I'm telling her, "We're looking good. We're in a good spot." It helps my nerves explaining the race like that. It's like an outlet.

Coming to the three-eighths pole, I see that he's moving well, and we're all starting to get excited. Turning for home, I say to myself, "He's gonna hit the board." Now I'm really getting excited. He's gonna run third or fourth. This is great. Then, Unbridled's Song begins to drift out to the middle of the track, and Cavonnier starts moving — fourth, third, second. All of a sudden, he takes the lead at the eighth pole. I was not prepared mentally for that. You think you are, but when it really happens, you realize you're not. Again I'm going, "Oh my God! I can't believe this." And we just explode in the box. My whole life is now flashing before my eyes. I'm pleading with God to give it to me. I'm promising to go to church every day. You just can't describe the feeling. It's like an out-of-body experience.

I look back to see what's happening, and there's one horse coming at us. I check where the wire is. I'm thinking, "Come on, get there already." When I look back, I see that it's the Overbrook colors, so I know it's a good one. He's coming and coming, and I can tell that Chris doesn't see him. But he never stops riding Cavonnier. When they hit the wire together, I was at a bad angle, and Grindstone was so far out in the middle of the track. From the angle, I honestly thought Cavonnier had hung on. I couldn't

17

believe it. I turned around, and everyone's telling me I got it. I'm asking everyone around us, "Did we get it? Did we get it?" Bob Walter, the owner of Cavonnier, said he thought we got it.

Just then, Sherry turns to me and says, "I think we ran second." I mean, I wanted to shake her when she said that. I'm saying, "What the hell do you know? You don't even go to the races. Don't even think second." Mrs. Walter then turns around and she puts two fingers up because she also thought we had run second. I felt like cutting her fingers off. Meanwhile, it's taking forever, and I'm trying to look at the expressions on the jockeys' faces. I'm looking at McCarron, and he's not sure. I look at Bailey on Grindstone, and he's smiling a little bit. I don't like that. Now I'm starting to get bad vibes. At this point, I'm thinking, "Come on already, somebody tell me what's going on."

They showed the replay, and I still couldn't tell. Finally, I started to prepare myself for the worst. Maybe I got beat. I decided to stay in the box and not go down until the photo came up. I just didn't want to be down there. By the time they finally hung the numbers up, I was fully prepared for the worst. When they put Grindstone's number up I just went numb. Somebody came over to me and I remember saying, "Well, at least for a few minutes I knew what it felt like to win the Kentucky Derby."

As soon as they hung the numbers up, I told Sherry, "Let's go down. You come with me." I started going down the stairs, and, wham! it hit me all at once. If someone had come over to me at that point, I would have broken down and cried. Just then, I saw William T. Young coming down with his daughter, Lucy, and I congratulated him. We were both in the same fraternity in college, Sigma Alpha Epsilon, and I slipped him the secret grip. He was so excited and thanked me. And as much as I hated to lose and hated to get beat by

D. Wayne Lukas, at least here was a good man who had won. He was just the chosen one this year.

It was when I got down there, and listened to Chris being interviewed by Leslie Visser, that I learned that Cavonnier had gotten whipped across the face turning for home. Leslie was just about to start talking to me, when they ran out of time and switched away. I couldn't believe it. This was my big opportunity to be on ABC, and they stiffed me.

After the race, Dick Vitale, the college basketball analyst, came back to the barn to see the horse, and he tells me how tough it must be to lose like that. Then he asks me how they know about the photo. He says, "If I owned or trained that horse, I would demand to see the photo before they put it up. I'd make a stink about it." I told him it doesn't work that way. Then he makes me feel even better by telling me, "That race could have made you. That's like getting beat at the buzzer." All I said to him was, "That's exactly right."

Meanwhile, all the media was around Unbridled's Song's trainer, Jim Ryerson. When they came to me, I told them I had been a Quarter Horse trainer, and instead of training him to go a mile and a quarter, I trained him to go a mile and 440 yards. I just came up a yard short. So, it was good at least that I was able to joke about it.

Earlier in the day, the Walters had a Monsignor come to the barn to bless the horse. Cavonnier was stabled next to Criollito, and when the Monsignor came back to the barn afterward, I told him he had blessed the wrong horse by mistake. And he's telling me, "No I didn't, Bob, I'm sure of it." Even he was upset. I think he did a little cursing after the race. One thing about the Monsignors, they will go to the window.

That night we all went to dinner at Pat's Steak House, and I was feeling pretty good. I saw Semoran's owner, Don Dizney, and his group, and they were all down because their horse had finished up the track. I could sympathize with them, but they had a good time at the Derby. Don told me, "Now I know what it feels like to run a horse in the Derby. Next time, I want to come with one I can win it with."

All of a sudden, while I was having dinner, it hit me like a ton of bricks. We all became super depressed. We were really bummed out. I showed up the next day and went over to congratulate Wayne, because I never saw him after the race. He was talking to the media, and I just told him what a great race it was.

I remember getting a call from Mike Pegram, and he was sick. He told me he threw a whole beer against the wall, he was so mad. Everybody who considered me a friend was sick about the whole thing. They all knew what I was thinking. I was convinced this was my only chance. I'll never be back. I don't have these kind of horses. I believe you get one big break in life, and you better take advantage of it. This was my one big break and I missed it.

The day after the race, I talked to Mr. Walter, and he asked me what I wanted to do. I told him the horse was pretty tired, and I thought we should go home and forget about the Preakness. He had just run his guts out, and I wasn't sure if I wanted to run him back in two weeks. But Mr. Walter said if the horse was okay, he wanted to try for the Preakness.

You hate to second-guess, but Cavonnier just wasn't the same horse at Pimlico. Meanwhile, the Monsignor showed up again, and he got us all together — McCarron and everybody — and had us all put our hands together while he said a prayer. "Lord, let us have a safe trip and win this race, blah, blah, blah." But in the race, Cavonnier was tired and really wasn't into the bit. Nick Zito's horse, Louis Quatorze, was out there cruising on the lead, but Cavonnier was just jumping up and down. He was floundering out there. ABC had miked me for the race, and I figured if the horse didn't run well, at least I'd get a little bit of exposure. But when I saw that we were going nowhere, I said into the mike, "Houston, we have a problem." And I'm telling you what, those ABC guys jerked that equipment off me so fast. You know you're in trouble and have no shot to win when they start taking the mike off you at the sixteenth pole.

Even though Cavonnier finished fourth in the Preakness, we decided to run him in the Belmont. I figured if he didn't train well I was going to go home with him. If he did train well, I was going to run. As it turned out, he trained super, so we kept going with him. I wanted to win one of these, and we felt, maybe the Belmont was going to be our race.

The horse looked great in the paddock. But then, here came the Monsignor again, and he wants McCarron to carry a crucifix in his saddle. I told him it was too big and there was no place to put it.

Cavonnier breaks well and he's in a good spot. Going around the turn, he starts making a move, and I yell, "Here he comes." All of a sudden, I start shaking. I'm actually trembling from the excitement, and I can't see a damn thing. Just then, in the corner of my eye, I see a horse pulling up on the outside. It's him. I couldn't tell if he was okay or not, so I ran down to the track, and I'm frantic at this point. I was going to run up there to the head of the stretch, but it was just too far. I'm asking the people down there, "What do you hear? What's wrong with him? How bad is it?" No one knows anything.

Then McCarron finally comes back, and he says, "Man, it's bad, Bob." I'm thinking the worst, that the sesamoids are gone. They cart him off in the ambulance, and I'm walking back to the barn myself, saying, "Please, Lord, please don't let it be the sesamoids. A pulled suspensory, anything, but not that." All I'm thinking is that if I have to put this horse down, it'll kill me. He's such a neat little horse. All the way back, I'm saying some heavy-duty prayers.

I got back to the barn and the vet is already looking at him. I asked him what it looked like, and he looks at me and says, "It's a high bow." I go, "Oh, thank God. It's only a (bowed) tendon." He may never run again, but at this point I don't care. We iced him and took care of him, and he just stood there calmly. What a tough horse he was. And he had so much heart. We stayed with him and showed him all the love we could. I got so emotional. I just stood there petting him, and said, "Buddy, I'm sorry I put you through all this."

A short while later, McCarron came back to see how the horse was doing, and we all got to talking about the Monsignor. My good friend Brad McKenzie, who my mother calls the fifth and nicest Baffert brother, was there and says, "I think we need to send the Monsignor to the Lukas camp. He's killing us." We all break up laughing, and that helped break the tension.

New York left a bad taste in my mouth that day. Not so much because of the injury, but because they changed the track two days before the Belmont. It was loose and deep, and the injury Cavonnier suffered comes from that kind of track. That's what I was upset about.

So, we packed up and left the next day, and from then on, I was just thinking, there was my Triple Crown. It was long and it was grueling. But it was fun in the beginning, and at least we got a little bit of action out of it.

After the Derby, I was convinced I had blown it and would never be back. But little did I know that a two-year-old I had purchased privately a week earlier would change the course of my life.

A SILVER LINING

"My brother Kevin and I met Bob at the Keeneland September sales, and we just started shootin' the bull. I knew he was a California trainer who was doing good out there, but most of all, he was the guy who was really gettin' in our hair every time we tried to buy a horse. After he outbid us on High Stakes Player, I went up to him afterward and said, 'You know, why don't you just get the hell out of here. If you just leave, I'll upgrade your ticket to first class.' And he said to me, 'I'm already flying first class, buddy.' From then on, we kind of hit it off and discussed how we brought our young horses along. We had no idea what it was going to lead to, but even in the beginning, we'd send horses out to Bob in California and they'd take off. We'd send him good horses, but he made them even better than we thought they were. I remember when we found Silver Charm for him. Man was I pissed when I couldn't get a hold of him. Here I was working my ass off, and I felt like he was blowing me off. The cool thing about it was when I did get in touch with him after he watched the video, it was, 'Buy the horse.' No questions asked. And for a couple of days we actually did own that sonofagun." — *J. B. McKathan*

I really believe in fate, and Silver Charm made me even more of a believer. If it hadn't been for fate, I never would have been looking for a horse at the Ocala sale in April of 1996. If it hadn't been for a client whose wife freaked out over seeing a horse break down in front of her, Silver Charm definitely would have had another owner and trainer. I truly believe it was fate that brought us all together.

It started in August of 1995, when I took on a client named Malley Cornell, a really nice guy from San Diego. He was in the trucking business and at one time had about fifty horses, but was down to one horse and he was looking for a trainer, so he gave the horse to me.

He was trying to get back in the business, but his wife was really turned off by racing. They had had a few horses break down, and she really couldn't handle it. I wound up breaking the horse's maiden at Del Mar in '95, and after that race, Malley took Sherry and me out to dinner. We talked about racing and had a really good time.

The next morning, Malley brings his wife out to watch the workouts. We're near the five-eighths pole when a two-year-old filly who happened to be owned by Bob Lewis and trained by Wayne Lukas snaps her leg off right in front of us and goes down. I mean it was ugly. Of all the times for this to happen…I couldn't believe it. The filly just took a bad step and broke her cannon bone. It was one of those things that unfortunately happens.

Malley's wife leaves in tears, and he says, "Oh man, can you believe this? I really had her coming around." The following year, he calls me and says, "You know, Bob, if you happen to find a nice two-year-old in one of the horses-in-training sales in the $50,000 to $100,000 range, I might be interested. Give me first crack at it." He was still hopeful he'd be able to get his wife to come around.

In April of 1996, I went to Keeneland and saw a Summer Squall colt who was a full brother to Othello, a Lukas colt who finished second in the 1995 Del Mar Futurity. I liked the colt and knew he had worked well, so I called Padrig Campion, a friend of my assistant Eoin Harty. He owned a breeding farm in Lexington, and I asked him if he'd go out to the sale and see what the Summer Squall might bring. Padrig ended up buying the colt for $80,000, but when we X-rayed him after the sale, it turned out he had a fractured sesamoid. Luckily, the consignor took him back, but that scared the hell out of me because my name was on the sales ticket for a horse I hadn't vetted. I swore to the Lord, "Please, Lord, get me out of this and I'll never do this again."

I told Malley the horse didn't vet out, but I'd be looking at the Ocala (Florida) two-year-olds in training sale that was coming up later in April. I then called J. B. McKathan. J. B. and his brother, Kevin, broke my horses in Florida and were my contacts at the sales. I asked J. B. what he liked, and he said there were three horses: a gray filly, a gray Silver Buck colt, and a colt by Candi's Gold. I told him to send me a tape of the two grays. I wasn't interested in the Candi's Gold, no matter what he looked like.

The Silver Buck colt had been bought as a yearling at Ocala for $16,500 by Randy Hartley and Dean De Renzo (Florida-based pin-hookers who specialize in reselling young horses), then sold privately before the April sale to Tim Gardiner, a jockey in Canada who breaks horses for J. B.

Gardiner had worked the horse and really liked him. He advised one of his clients, C. J. Gray, to buy him privately for $30,000. Gray bought him, then decided to wheel him right back in the April sale to try to make a quick profit. The colt worked a quarter before the sale in :21⅘, and really caught J. B.'s eye.

I was at Churchill Downs at the time, getting Cavonnier ready for the Derby. Right before the Ocala sale, I had to fly from Louisville to Phoenix to saddle The Texas Tunnel, owned by Mike Pegram, in the Great Arizona Futurity Shoot-Out Trial. I called J. B. from Phoenix and asked him to send a tape of the Silver Buck colt to the Executive West in Louisville, where I was staying.

The day after the race in Arizona, we headed back to Louisville, but we got stuck in St. Louis for four hours because of the snow, and I blew any chance I had of getting back in time to see the tape before the sale. When I finally got to Louisville and saw the tape, I fell in love with the colt. I called up J. B. the next morning, and I said, "J. B., I love that horse. Damn it." He turned out just a little, but I loved the way he worked and the way he moved, and he just had that look about him. I asked J. B. what the colt brought, and he told me the consignor thought we were going to buy him and that there'd be a lot of action on him, so they ran the price up and wound up having to buy him back for $100,000.

I asked J. B. what they wanted for the colt, and they said they were looking for $80,000. I told J. B., "I'll tell you what I'll do. I'll give them $80,000 and I'll give you guys $5,000." J. B. says OK and asks me who I'm buying the colt for. I tell him I'm going to buy him for this guy Malley Cornell.

So I call Malley and tell him I got this Silver Buck colt. I mention that the bottom side's not all that great, and I fax him the pedigree and tell him he's a real good horse and I love him. He calls me back and says the pedigree is a little weak. I tell him not to worry about that. I assure him he's a good horse. But I could tell he wasn't that enthused. I said to him, "If you don't like him, don't worry about it, I'll get him sold."

I figured if I told him that and gave him an out, he'd really jump at the deal. Well, he didn't jump at it. The next day, Malley calls and says, "Bob, I just talked to my accountant, and he said if I sold my stock right now, I'd lose money on it, and it would be a bad investment to buy this horse."

J. B. loved this horse so much, he suggested the two of us just partner up on him. I wasn't in a position to do it at the time, but believe me, I would have bought the sonofabitch myself. I call J. B. and tell him the guy bailed out on me, and J. B. goes, "Shit, what are we going to do?" Right now, we're the owners of the horse.

The next day, I'm at Churchill Downs and I see Buzz Chace, who buys horses for several clients in addition to Ernie Paragallo. Buzz had shown a lot of interest in the Silver Buck colt himself, but didn't buy him. I ask him if he's interested, and he tells me, "Well, I like the horse. Maybe I can get Ernie to buy him and we can send him to you in California." He says Ernie is coming in the following morning and he's sure he'll go for it. We start joking around, and I even talk about renaming him. Being he was by Silver Buck out of a Poker mare, I said, "Let's name him Poker for a Buck."

I came back to the barn that afternoon, and I find out Unbridled's Song is dead lame. The next morning, they're all down there and they're soaking his foot, the whole deal. I go over to Buzz, and I say, "I know you're having some bad luck over there, but what about that colt? Did you talk to Ernie?" He says, "Forget it. Forget it. This isn't the time. Sell it to somebody else. I don't even want to bring it up."

I could have gone to Mike Pegram, but he had so many horses at the time, and I always bought him yearlings, not two-year-olds. I just didn't want to bug him. Then I noticed a note I had left for myself to call Bob Lewis and give him an update on Criollito.

I hadn't really done any good for Bob in the past. I had bought horses for him, but we just didn't have much luck. I felt I was getting squeezed out. I wasn't feeling the love from Bob that I once did. He told me a year earlier that I was winning races for other people, but not for him. Criollito was doing good, but Bob just didn't trust me to spend a lot of money for him. He had Lukas as his big spender. He liked me a lot, but I just felt the respect wasn't there.

Anyway, I called Bob and we talked about Criollito. I felt this was my last chance to get a good horse for him, so I just mentioned to him that I had bought this two-year-old and I really loved him, and I was looking for a buyer for him. I told him his pedigree isn't that great, but he's a runner and he worked beautiful. Bob says, "How much are we talking about?" I tell him, "It's $85,000 — eighty for the horse and five for J. B. and Kevin McKathan." Bob just says nonchalantly, "Sure, if you like him, go ahead. What are you going to do with him?" I told him I was going to bring him to California and get him ready for Del Mar. "Excellent," he says. "That's great. We've got a horse."

I told him one thing we've got to do first is change his name. He asks me what it is, and I tell him, Silver Charm. "Do you think that's too feminine?" he asks. I said, "No, but because he's by Silver Buck out of a Poker mare, I'd like to change it to Poker for a Buck." I was really pushing for that name. Bob starts laughing and says, "Well, I don't think Beverly will go for that, Bob."

So that's how Bob Lewis came to own Silver Charm. If that two-year-old filly of Bob's didn't break down in front of Malley Cornell's wife, he never would have had Silver Charm. And neither would I, because I would have bought horses for Malley in September and wouldn't even have been looking for a horse at Ocala the following April.

But fate wasn't through with us just yet.

LUCKY CHARM

"One of the reasons Bobby has gotten to where he is so fast is that he's a quick study. He'll admit when he screws up, and you can bet he won't screw up the same way twice. He doesn't do anything but train hors es, read racing publications, and watch racing tapes. He lives, eats, and breathes horse racing. It was his learning experience with Cavonnier that got Silver Charm there the following year. And it was his learning experi- ence with Silver Charm that helped Real Quiet. When Bobby made the transition to Thoroughbreds, he always had it in his mind he was going to train top-class stakes horses, and he always had it in his mind he was going to win the Kentucky Derby." — Brad McKenzie

Silver Charm arrived at my barn at Santa Anita shortly after the Ocala sale. And although he worked pretty decent, he was a lazy sonofagun. We went to Del Mar, and I worked him from the gate one day, and he went six furlongs in 1:10⅗. I mean, he was smokin'. That's racehorse time, especially for an unraced two-year- old. So now I knew this horse could really run.

I decide to unleash him on Pacific Classic Day in a six-furlong maiden race with David Flores up. Cigar is in the big race, trying to break Citation's modern-day record of sixteen straight wins, and I'm going to show this horse off. I'm already thinking of getting back to the Kentucky Derby. I'm just hoping I can find a horse who will get me there. Even though he hadn't run, I'm thinking this might be the

29

one. The track was pretty deep that day, and he got out there and was cookin'. Then Lukas' horse, Deeds Not Words, comes out of the clouds and gallops right by him and beats him by four lengths. Another horse, by Summer Squall, closes like crazy and looks as impressive as the winner. When they hit the wire, I'm thinking, "Man, was I wrong about him." I thought he was a lot more horse than that. I really felt he was going to destroy those horses.

Then we watch Cigar get beat, and we're all bummed. It was a horrible day. I go back to the barn, and we scope Silver Charm, and it turns out he bled. That made me feel a little better. I figured that's what got him beat. I come back and work him on Lasix, and, man, he worked great. So I run him again, and he's in against a real good maiden of Bob Lewis' named Gold Tribute, who Lukas paid $725,000 for. I had been watching him in the morning and he was working real good. Bob was up at Saratoga at the time, so I left a message for him, saying, "Bob, your horse is in, but he's up against your real expensive horse, Gold Tribute. I hate to do it to you, but I'm gonna kick your $725,000 horse's ass with my $80,000 dollar horse."

Wayne was also up at Saratoga, and he was watching the race with Bob, who told me later that Wayne had said to him, "Wait until you see this horse run." When they turned for home, Wayne says, "Here he comes. Now he's gonna show 'em." Just then, ol' Silver Charm kicks away from him and wins going away.

By this time, the Baffert-Lukas rivalry was in full gear. It was during Cavonnier's Triple Crown that I realized Wayne didn't like me. And I think it was the Bob Lewis deal that helped cause it. But I actually had Bob before Wayne did, and he was the one who asked me what Bob was like. I told him he was a great guy to work for, and when they eventually hooked up, I sort of got pushed out of the picture. I still trained a couple of horses for Bob, and that created a little bit of friction between Wayne and me. Before that, we had been friends. We talked every day.

When I came to Churchill with Cavonnier, I had accepted the fact that I had blown the Bob Lewis deal. But things just weren't the same between Wayne and me. I could see a difference in his attitude toward me. Then, the day of the Derby, Rick Bozich of the Louisville *Courier-Journal* really hosed me. Bozich had come over to me a couple of weeks before the race and asked me why I thought Wayne had five horses in the Derby. I told him, "The Derby is all about ego. These owners put all this money up and they want to be there. Take Semoran for example. I don't want to run him, but the owners are from Kentucky and they're all pumped up. And I'm sure that Wayne is in the same position."

I always respected Wayne. He came up the same way I did. He's a great horseman and won all these big races. My mistake in this instance was that I never read that article. After Criollito won the Churchill Downs Handicap, they took us up to the President's Room to toast us and drink champagne. We had all bet on the horse, and we were psyched. All of a sudden, Wayne comes walking in and he just glares at me and walks past me. I'm thinking, "What the hell was that all about?" Then, as I'm walking out, he comes up to me and says, "Why did you take that shot at me in the paper?"

I had been making fun of his cowboy hat all week, saying it was so big it would get caught in the elevator doors. So I thought he was referring to my jokes about his hat. He said no, it was the comment I made in Bozich's article that he was running five horses in the Derby because of ego. I told him I never said that, forgetting about my talk with Rick. Then he says to me, "You want to go toe to toe with me in the press, I'll go toe to toe with you." Here I had just won a stakes for Bob Lewis, and you just don't do that. I didn't even know what the hell he was talking about. Then, when I read the article, I realized that wasn't even what I told the guy. I said it, but it wasn't about Wayne, it was about the owners.

At the Preakness, I confronted Wayne, and I said to him, "Why are you so worried about me? I'm no threat to you. You just won the Derby, and I'm here with this damn Cal-bred, and you'll probably never see me back here again." After that, we never really had much to say to each other. It was too bad, because I really liked the guy at one time.

Anyway, I start training Silver Charm for the Del Mar Futurity. Right before the race, Bob Lewis comes to me and says he just received a fax from Lukas' guy Michael Tabor, who won the '95 Derby with Thunder Gulch. Tabor wants to buy Silver Charm for $500,000, and Bob asks me what I think. I told him, "I don't know; it's a lot of money. If he should stub his toe tomorrow, he'd be worth about $2,500 as a stallion. But I would still have to say no."

So Bob says, "Okay, we won't sell." Now I've got some pressure on me. I just talked the guy into turning down a half-million dollars.

I ran Silver Charm in the Del Mar Futurity and he's up against Gold Tribute again. Now the tension is really heating up between Wayne and me. He's at the Keeneland September sale with Bob Lewis watching on television, and I'm at the track with Beverly. They turn for home, and the two horses are nose and nose, and we beat him a head. Bob Lewis didn't even know who to root for. When he got back, I told him this was my Derby horse.

The next day, I went to Keeneland for the sale, and I saw Wayne walking by. I said to him, "Hey, Wayne, that was a helluva race, wasn't it?" He tells me, "Do you realize what you did? You just cost Bob Lewis about two or three million dollars." He said if I hadn't run Silver Charm in the race and he had won it with Gold

Tribute, a son of Mr. Prospector, the horse would have been worth about two or three million, while my horse doesn't have any pedigree. I told Wayne, "Well, if you want to make your horse worth two or three million dollars, you better get him the hell out of California." And that's what he did. He wound up sending Gold Tribute to New York, and although he ran a few good races, he never did much after that.

I was going to run Silver Charm next in the Norfolk Stakes, but he got sick on me. I could have run him in the Breeders' Cup Juvenile, but I told Bob, "This is my Derby horse. I'd like to back off and give him a little time, then get him ready for the three-year-old races. I want to get back to the Derby, and I've got a plan on how to get him there." Bob said fine. One thing about Bob, he trusts his trainers and lets them do whatever they want.

Before the Breeders' Cup, Bob calls me and says he just got another offer from the same people. This time, for $1.7 million. I told him, "We got to take it." And Bob says, "Okay, I'll tell them."

They send one of their guys, David Lambert, out to look at the horse at Santa Anita and perform a heart scan. They checked the heart and lungs, and it was good, but it wasn't a bull's-eye. Suddenly, I started getting seller's remorse. The next day, they were going to come out and watch him gallop. I called Bob Lewis and said, "I know I told you to sell, but did you sign anything that says we have to sell?" He said he didn't sign anything, but he thought maybe they were more interested in checking out the competition than actually buying the horse. I told him if I'm going to go back to the Derby, this may be my only shot. I said, "I know it's a lot of money, but I'm changing my mind about selling him."

Bob tells me to just wait and see what happens. So I get to the barn the next day and wait for them to come. Now I know Silver

Charm is the type of horse who doesn't look good galloping. He looks like he's stiff in the back and he goes real slow. That's just him. He's always been like that. I tell my exercise rider, Larry Damore, "Larry, I want you to make him look real shitty today. Don't even carry your stick. I don't want to sell this horse, but I want them to be the ones to back out. When he comes back, I'm going to ask you how he went, and I want you to say he felt okay, but not like he did at Del Mar. Maybe it's the track here. Say it usually takes him about a mile to warm out of it. Just don't go overboard. I don't want it to sound too obvious that we're trying to talk them out of it."

We're watching him gallop and he looks like shit. David Lambert is real good, but when they look at a horse, they want to see the obvious. He says to me, "He looks like he's a little stiff." I told him, "I think it's the track here, David. It always takes him a while to warm out of it. You should have seen him at Del Mar. But he's okay. He's sound."

Then Larry comes back, and I say, "So Larry, he went good?" And he says, "Yeah, like usual. It took him about a mile to warm up. He wasn't like he was at Del Mar. Maybe it's the track."

So now we had planted the seed. We go back to the barn, and by this time David Lambert is really giving it the heavy look. I tell him, "He can really run, but I just hope that goddamn pedigree doesn't show up. I even told Bob Lewis, one bad step and this sonofabitch is worth twenty-five hundred bucks."

A couple of days later, Bob Lewis calls and says, "Bob, you can relax. They faxed me back and said they're not interested. Thank you very much, but they're going to pass." And I go, "Yes!" Then I call David Lambert and ask him what happened. "Was it the heart scan?" I asked. He said, "No, it's okay, but I think about a mile to a mile and a sixteenth is his capability."

When I talked to David later, he told me it was the pedigree that scared the hell out of them. So we really dodged a bullet there. If that horse had gone to Lukas and won the Derby, I'd be done. I'd be working at one of Mike Pegram's McDonald's franchises. That would have cooked me for good. But once again, fate stepped in.

ON TOP OF THE WORLD

"It was like I had won the Derby that day. I had been there with Bobby from the beginning, and I had seen all the blood, sweat, and tears he put into the business. We had put in a lot of miles together, and I knew how hard he worked to get this. But you talk about fate, and how things work out in strange ways. I'm in a box up on the third floor, and I'm not anywhere near Bobby. How this wound up happening, I have no idea, but I went running down and hit that track the exact same time he did. I can remember, we looked at each other, and it was like, "How in the hell can we be here at the same time?" Me and Bobby and his brother Billy are standing there, and we're hugging each other right there on the track, and there isn't a dry eye among us. I'm convinced it was some sort of destiny, one that would come to an unbelievable climax for Bobby and me the following year."
— *Mike Pegram*

I hated to do it, but I went to David Flores before Silver Charm's first start at three, and I said to him, "David, I love you to death, but I want to go back to the Derby and I don't want to go with a rider who has never ridden in the race before. So I'm going to take you off the horse and put Chris McCarron on him." He was bummed out, but he understood.

I started getting him ready for the seven-furlong San Vicente on February 8, 1997, but he kept bleeding on me. That's why he was getting sick. He'd have a temperature for three days and we'd have to give him antibiotics. As we got closer to the race, I started getting nervous. He was the big horse, and he was coming back off a layoff, and he was going to be the favorite. And I was the one who really built him up. Plus, we turned down $1.7 million for him. So like I do before a big race, I got to leaking. It's an expression that means leaking confidence. First I'm telling Bob Lewis he's doing great, and now as the race gets closer, it's, "I don't know, man, it's a tough race." I mean, I'm leaking bad.

Bob has another horse trained by Wayne in the race, named Esteemed Friend, and we're running as an entry. Bob stays with Wayne, and Beverly sits in the box with me. They put Silver Charm in the gate and he breaks through. At first I'm pissed, but then I start thinking to myself, this is my out in case he doesn't run well. At the start, he breaks slow and he's behind horses for the first time. McCarron brings him up the rail, and all of a sudden, he opens up in the stretch. He gets a little tired at the end, but he wins by almost two lengths in 1:21. I turn to Beverly and I go, "Man, this is a good horse. I mean, this is a really good horse." I never had a horse do that. It was unbelievable.

We're all pumped up, and I go down to the winner's circle, and McCarron is telling me, "Man, Bob, he was really blowing hard when I pulled him up." Every time I'd work him, he'd always blow really hard because of his bleeding — just blow and blow, like he's dead tired. I just didn't know how much harder I could be on him.

I kept working him hard after the San Vicente, and I was going to run him in the San Rafael, but the Charm got sick on me again. He came down with a little temperature and I had to give him a few days off. I waited for the San Felipe on March 16, and this time he breaks well, and at the three-eighths pole I look at him and he's outside of horses and going nowhere. I can hear track announcer Trevor

Denman say, "And Silver Charm is hard-ridden to keep up." That's the death call. I don't know what's going on. I'm seeing my dream of getting back to the Derby dying right in front of me.

Just then, McCarron dove to the inside with him, and as soon as he did, the horse just took off on his own. He was flying down the stretch and finished second to Free House, beaten three-quarters of a length. Even McCarron came back and said it was amazing. It was like, "I don't know where it came from." But of course, he mentions that the horse was blowing real hard again.

Meanwhile, Ron McAnally had a horse named Hello who finished a fast-closing third in the San Rafael with McCarron aboard. I told Bob Lewis I think we might lose McCarron. Chris wanted to wait before making a decision, but Bob said he wanted to have a rider named for the Santa Anita Derby, so without a commitment from Chris, we named Gary Stevens.

A week before the Santa Anita Derby, I went to Turfway Park with Chris, who was riding Inexcessivelygood for me in the Jim Beam Stakes. The horse was on the lead in the stretch and broke down, and we had to have him euthanized right there. It was awful. Chris was pretty sore and bruised up and spent the night in the hospital. I stayed around and flew back to California with him the next day.

On the plane, I said to him, "You know, Chris, I got to ask you something. Why did you take off Silver Charm?" He told me, "I didn't take off him, you took me off." I said, "Look, I don't want to hear this bullshit, you didn't want to ride him. What was it?"

He said to me, "Bob, every time I worked him or after a race, he was blowing so hard that I feel he really doesn't want to go that far. I think seven-eighths is his max." I tried to explain that it was just him. The reason the Charm is breathing hard is that he bleeds. The horse must have had pneumonia or something when he was young, because we X-rayed his lungs and he had some scar tissue on one lung. It was either that or he once spent a summer in a Kentucky coal mine.

I had Gary work him after the San Felipe, and he went in :59 and change. He comes back, and of course is blowing hard. Gary goes, "Man, for a horse who just came off a mile and a sixteenth race, he feels like he's fit to go three-quarters of a mile. You haven't even come close to getting to the bottom of this horse." I liked hearing that. If he could do the things he did without being fit, what's going to happen when I did get him fit?

When I got back from Turfway, I worked him six furlongs and told Gary, "I want you to put a helluva work in him. I want you whippin' him." And Gary loved that. These jocks love when you tell them that. The horse worked in 1:10⅘, and Gary asked, "How was that?" and I said, "That's what I was looking for." I called Bob Lewis and said, "Now Bob, I don't want you to panic, but he just worked in ten and one. People are going to tell you stuff, but don't worry about it. He needed it."

On the morning of the Santa Anita Derby, I was listening to the Roger Stein radio show while driving to the track at 8 o'clock, and he's got Wayne on. Wayne was running Sharp Cat in the race against the boys, and he's saying that he's got a great shot in the race and how she's Derby material. One thing about Wayne, he's very convincing, and he convinced me he was going to win the Santa Anita Derby with that filly, because everyone was going to let her loose on the lead.

So I say to myself, "I'm not going to have any of that." I really hadn't given Free House the respect he deserved. When I got to the paddock before the race, I went up to Gary and said, "I want you to put it to the bitch. I want you to go toe-to-toe with her and run her into the ground." I wanted to get a good, hard race into Silver

Charm to get him ready for the Kentucky Derby, and he was so tough, I knew turning for home he'd gut it out of her.

Down the backstretch, the two of them are at each other's throat and really smokin'. Kent Desormeaux on Free House saw what was happening and he eased off. Gary told me later, when Kent eased off, he was going to ease off, too, but that bitch was doing it easy, he started thinking, if he did take back, I was going to be screaming at him. When I saw those fractions — :45, 1:09 — I'm thinking, "Oh my God, what did I do?"

Coming to the quarter pole, Sharp Cat was done. She was asking for the check. Then I see Free House coming and I knew I was going to get beat a block. All I'm thinking is, "What a stupid idiot I am." Free House lopes on by him, and I'm just hoping he can hold on for second. All of a sudden, Gary switches to his left-hand stick and Silver Charm kicks it back in again. He starts coming back at Free House and just gets beat a head, and one more jump he's going to get him. I lost the Santa Anita Derby, but I was thrilled. I was going back to the Kentucky Derby. Back to the old Twin Spires. I ran down to the track, and I was so happy, it was like I had won it.

I told Gary, "Man, did I blow it. I never should have sent him after her. But you know what, we may have lost the battle, but we're gonna win the war. I've never had a horse who came back like that."

When I arrived at Churchill Downs ten days before the Derby I really wasn't into the race. I was back, but I didn't have the same excitement as I had with Cavonnier. It just wasn't new to me anymore. Then I got invited to have lunch at the Kentucky Derby Museum. But I really didn't want to go into the museum itself. I felt I didn't want to go there unless I was in there. While we were having lunch, the big slide show came on in the museum. I had never seen the updated version, which included the '96 Derby. So I went in, and I was listening to the call of the race. "That's Cavonnier in front, and they hit the wire..." The music is building to this incredible climax, and it was like seeing an old girlfriend again. It brought that whole miserable feeling right back in my body.

I left there, and I said to myself, "I've got to win this race. If it takes me the rest of my life, I've got to win this race." From that point on, I became as focused as I've ever been on anything in my life.

When I first saw April Mayberry, who ran our stable there, I said to her, "April, I'm back with another one. But this time, I've got a lot more horse. And I'll tell you right now, if he gets headed, nobody's gonna pass this dude. He's got what it takes."

But we did have that same problem with him in the mornings. Every time I worked him, he'd bleed. And the word got out. Whenever anybody would say, "Hey, I hear your horse bled," I'd just hem and haw and not really say anything. He'd never bleed through the nostrils. It was just when you scoped him that you could see he bled. So, I had to give him Lasix every time I worked him, and he bled right through the Lasix.

On the Tuesday before the Derby, I just gave him a little easy five-eighths work. Afterward, I told the vet, "Doc, I want you to scope him, but when you take it out, I want you to say, 'It looks good.' And I'll talk to you later about it, and you can tell me what you saw." There were some people around, and I didn't want anyone to know because it had gotten out he was bleeding, and I didn't know where the leak was.

So he scoped him, and I asked him what he thought. "Good," he said. "Looks good." I walked him to his car, and I asked him, "Did it really look good?" He told me, "It looked terrible. He bled, he's got mucous, I mean it looked horrible."

This was the first time he had ever scoped him, and I said, "Doc, relax, will you. He always bleeds. Don't worry, I've been through this before. He'll run big." So he gave him some antibiotics just for the one day. You can't keep them on antibiotics because it weakens them and knocks their blood count down. My main worry was that he would get sick right before the Derby. I mean I was on pins and needles. That was his real problem and I was just living in fear the days leading up to the race.

The morning of the race I was still worried. Every few minutes, it was, "Take his temperature," "How's he doing?"

The day was cold and miserable, but Bob Lewis had heard so much about the walk that he wanted to do it anyway. It was a different walk than the previous year. This was a serious walk. The first time, it was the excitement and "I can't believe I'm here." But this time, it was "We've got to win this thing. Here I am lucky enough to get a second chance the very next year. I can't blow it this time. This really could be my last chance."

The fans were cheering me on, and you could tell they really wanted me to win. Silver Charm looked great. Nothing bothered or excited him. One thing about this horse, he is so cool. He's got ice water in his veins. I looked up and I saw one of the contenders, Pulpit, and he was doing the Mexican hat dance in front of us. He was jumping and rearing and getting all hot. I could see all these horses falling apart in front of me, and Silver Charm was quiet and relaxed. I told my brothers, "I hope he's not getting a temperature on me right now."

But as soon as he made the turn to go into the tunnel, he started to coil a little and flex his muscles. When he does that, I know he's on. I said, "I like that. That's a good sign." I saddled him up and told Gary, "Just make that move and get us to the front at the eighth pole." I could tell Gary was really pumped. I said to him, "Just go out there and do what you got to do. And if we don't make it, we'll just bring another one next year."

You always worry about the break, and when the gate opened and he came out clean, I breathed a sigh of relief. Free House was on the lead coming by us and we were in a great position. Going around the clubhouse turn it started to get hairy. I truly believe this race is won or lost on the first turn. Position is everything. I could see this spot in front of him and it was starting to close. Gary saw what was happening and just gunned him right through there. That was the winning deal right there. He rode aggressively and went for the spot. If he hadn't, who knows where he would have wound up.

He got through that little jam great and was in a perfect spot down the backside. Pulpit was out there on the lead, and we were just cruising along behind him. At the three-eighths pole, Silver Charm started moving, and when they're moving at the three-eighths pole it means they're running their race. I knew at this point we were going to be one, two, three, and I started getting excited.

Bob is next to me in the box and I'm telling him what's going on. We had better seats this time and I had a better angle of the finish. "We're okay, Bob. We're in a perfect spot," I tell him. They come to the quarter pole, and I say, "We're moving now." That was it. At that point, there was no more explaining the race. I just started riding that horse myself. I'm yelling, "Come on!" over and over again. I could see Free House is starting to get tired, and we go by him. All of a sudden, I look back and I see that damn Captain Bodgit flying on the outside. He was the favorite and was coming off impressive wins in the Florida Derby and Wood Memorial, so I know we've got a fight on our hands. As Captain Bodgit starts closing the gap, I go "Oh man, not again. Lord, you can't do this to me again."

But this time I felt different. I had a real confident feeling. I keep thinking, "He's not going to let that horse get by him. There is no way he's going to let him get by him." I just felt if he did let him get by, he deserved to lose the race. Just then, Captain Bodgit comes to him and pulls up alongside him. I could see Silver Charm digging in and fighting back, and I'm screaming. When they hit that wire and he had his head in front, I just wanted to jump out of my body. I looked up and I couldn't believe it. I grabbed Bob and I almost broke him in half shaking him.

I don't even remember how I got down to the track. All I do remember is stepping out on the track and seeing Mike Pegram. I ran up to Mike and grabbed him and hugged him. "I can't believe we did it," I said to him. Although it wasn't Mike's horse, I felt he was part of it, and so did he. The McKathan brothers were down there and we were absolutely going crazy.

But my family was still in the box. My friend Brad McKenzie was with them and told them to wait for the photo before they went down. When they took the winner's circle photo, we were all so excited we didn't even realize they weren't even in the picture. As it turned out, they wouldn't let them across the track because there were too many people. There was P. A., my sisters Norie and Dee Dee, and friends from Arizona, and they couldn't get to the winner's circle.

When ABC interviewed me, all I kept thinking about was Mike Pegram and how he got me in the Thoroughbred business. I always thanked him for that. And he'd tell me, "You know what? The day you win the Kentucky Derby, you can thank me then." I always remembered that, and it hit me when I was standing up there. So when Jim McKay started talking to me, I thanked Mike on national TV, and I ended it by saying, "So, Mike, this one's for you, my man."

Afterward, Mike told several people, "I've only cried twice in my life: when my father died and when Bobby won the Kentucky

Derby." Everyone would ask him why I didn't buy the horse for him, and he'd say it was because that horse was meant for Bob Lewis. Little did he know that his horse was right there in the barn, waiting in the wings.

Then there was Brad McKenzie, who's like a brother to me. I looked down at Brad and he was crying like a baby. It was so emotional. The beauty of it is that friends from all over the country who I went to college with all called and congratulated me. One friend of mine who I hadn't seen in years told me as soon as the race was over, some girl we knew from school called him and said, "Do you believe it? Do you believe Bobby Baffert, that clown we went to school with, just won the Kentucky Derby?"

After the race, we all went to the Derby Museum for the post-race party. They toasted us, and Bob Lewis and I hugged each other. Then they showed the slide presentation from the previous year. I watched it again, and you know what? It didn't bother me at all this time. All those feelings that had gnawed at me for a whole year were completely gone.

All I kept thinking that night was, "I did it! My life is fulfilled."

I slept like a rock that night. The next morning, I was flying high as I drove into the backstretch. I could see all the media at the barn waiting for me, so I went around the other way. The first thing I did was stop at Captain Bodgit's barn and talk with his trainer, Gary Capuano. He was such a nice kid, and I told him, "I know what you're feeling. It's tough, but for what it's worth, you did one helluva job with that horse. I never thought I'd be back, but here I am just a year later. What's important is that you showed everyone you could do it."

I then drove to the barn from the opposite direction so no one would see me, and I came tearing around there honking my horn. Everyone was there laughing. It was just an unforgettable feeling.

The following morning, however, things got a little weird. I had a horse running in the Great Arizona Futurity Shoot-Out for Mike again, and I had told him, "I'm not going to Turf Paradise. You're on your own. I'm staying right here to gloat and soak it all in."

At about ten o'clock, I'm buying T-shirts at the half-price sale, and I assume Mike was on his way. I get a phone call and it's Mike. He had had a girlfriend with him at the Derby and she had given him a gift and told him to open it before he left. But he never did.

"Bahama," he says. That's what he called me. "It's Mike. I'm in jail." I ask him where he is and what happened, and he says, "Ah, that damn goofy broad. Remember I told you she gave me a gift? Well, I never opened it and it turned out to be a goddamn gun, so they got me locked up." He said the girl was trying to get a lawyer, but I told him I'd try to get a hold of Governor Jones. The governor, Brereton Jones, was a top Thoroughbred owner and breeder, and I figured he'd be able to help out. I reached him, but he was just about ready to leave for church. He said he'd try to make some calls.

Just then, Buck Wheat drives up. He's the director of horsemen's relations at Churchill Downs. I told him the story, and Buck says, "Don't worry, I'll take care of it. I got a buddy down there." So he calls this Capt. Steve Thompson and he goes down there and within twenty minutes he had Mike out and delivered him to my barn. Mike had also won a lot of money betting Silver Charm, so when they arrested him, he had this large wad of bills in his pocket and a gun in his bag. After that, we started calling the girl "Annie Oakley."

One thing about Mike, he's very superstitious. He'll go out with a girl, and if he's kickin' ass winning races, he keeps bringing that girl, even if he can't stand her. He was doing real well with this girl. He kept saying, "I'm telling you Bob, we're on a roll with her. We won the Derby and we won some other races." I said, "Let me tell you what. We're on a roll because we're on a roll. If you think it's because of some girl, you're crazy." So that day, they split up. She was out of the picture. I took Mike to the airport, and I told him, "Look, that girl is out. We got Holy Nola in the Great Arizona Futurity Shoot-Out, and the race is getting ready to run right now. We'll find out if we're on a roll because of her." I call up for the result and Holy Nola wins by a length. "See, what did I tell you?" I said. "We're on a roll."

It was nice going to the Preakness. It was a mellow deal and we were on top. The pressure was off. The only hang-up there was when somebody left my two-way radio on all night, and when I worked Silver Charm the next morning, the radio was dead and I had no communication with the rider. I kept saying it was sabotage, but the more I look back, I think I was the one who did it. As it turned out, he worked sluggishly that day, but I made up for it in his gallops. Of course, he bled after the Derby, just like he always did. When I saw Gary, I told him he was going to be a little short for the race, and if he won it wasn't going to be by much. I really didn't crank on him at all.

In the Preakness, I really thought he was beaten. He wasn't going to get by Free House in the stretch, but then Captain Bodgit came charging up on his outside, and when he heard him, he took off again and just got his head in front at the wire. I thought for sure he got beat. I couldn't see the finish well, and I told Bob Lewis I thought he lost. But Bob kept telling me, "No, trust me, we won." We're arguing back and forth like Mutt and Jeff, and finally, Bob turned to Nick Zito, who was right behind us and said, "Tell him, Nick. Tell him we won." And Nick said we got it.

After the race, I didn't even scope him. I didn't want to know anymore. It was driving me crazy, so I quit scoping him.

We came back to Churchill Downs, and people stopped me wherever I went. I was signing buttons, napkins, anything they could find. That was really weird, signing things. To me, I'm no celebrity. The horses are the celebrities. I never did take myself seriously, and I think that's why people could relate to me. I was just an ordinary guy who got lucky and was having fun, and I believe that's the reason people rooted for me and wanted to see me win.

One night at the Executive West, this family was having a big family reunion. I just sort of walked by and looked in the room to see what was going on. When they spotted me, they brought me in and started taking pictures of everyone with me, and having me sign autographs. The next thing I know, I'm mingling with everybody, talking about the Derby.

I was doing a local radio show the day before Silver Charm's workout on June 3. He was scheduled to leave for Belmont the day after the work. I kidded around, inviting the people to come out to the track to watch the work, which didn't sit very well with Churchill Downs. But I never thought they'd take me seriously. I couldn't believe it. The next day, the cars are pouring into the track. Thousands of people are gathered on the apron and there are huge crowds by the barn.

It almost turned into a disaster. When Silver Charm was heading past the stands, the crowd went wild and another horse going in the opposite direction got spooked by all the commotion and bolted right in his path. Luckily, we just missed him.

We finally left for Belmont and a chance at the Triple Crown. What a killer that was. We drove to the track ahead of the van, and when I got there I couldn't believe the crowd of reporters and photographers. That was the first time I'd been overwhelmed by the media. They were pushing and shoving and fighting. The way they attacked me, you'd have thought I was holding Monica Lewinsky's dress.

The whole experience was unbelievable. Bob Lewis had flown in some 200 friends and family members on a jumbo jet. And the poor guy came down with a bad case of bronchitis and was a sick sonofa-gun. He had just run himself down. We were really worried about him.

Before the race, it was wild. They drew a huge crowd, one of the largest ever, and they were all cheering me when I got in the box. Then I hear this incredible roar from below. I thought they were going in the gate, but someone told me, "No, all these people have been waiting for you." I wanted to do something for them. We had made up these buttons which read, "Bet the Farm on the Charm." I leaned over and they all let out this roar again. I felt like the Pope. I said, "I got to feed these guys." So I started grabbing these buttons and flinging them down into the crowd and they all went nuts.

I needed that $500,000 bonus money, which was ten percent of the Triple Crown's $5-million bonus to the winning owner. But when he got beat, I didn't think about that. It's like you're just glad it's all over. What was disappointing was truly believing that if he had seen Touch Gold, he would have dug down and found more. But Free House was screening him and he just never saw the horse. He was beaten three-quarters of length for the Triple Crown, but I still was on a high from winning the Derby, and this didn't hurt as badly as Cavonnier getting beat the year before.

Despite the problems and getting beat in the Belmont, we enjoyed every minute of it. I look back and say, "At least I got this far." Afterward, I thought back to flying on the plane to Belmont with Silver Charm, and Mike Pegram was with me. We were sitting on an ice chest, and Mike said to me, "One thing about all this. I might never get this far myself, but at least I know what it feels like to go through the Triple Crown." Little did he know that one year later, we'd be sitting on that same ice chest heading to Belmont again. But this time he would really know what it felt like.

RANCHO BAFFERT

"Bobby was never depressed or negative about anything. He always saw the bright side of life. Ever since he was a little kid, he had very high self-esteem and felt as if he was the greatest. I really believe it was that optimistic outlook that helped him become the success he has. He dealt with people at an early age, selling eggs for his father, and it was the skills he learned doing that which enabled him to deal so well with people later in life." — Ellie Baffert

I grew up in Nogales, Arizona, a neat little town located directly across the border from Nogales, Mexico. The population was about 6,000, compared to almost 20,000 now. Back then, everybody knew everybody, and it was just a great place to grow up.

My mother, Ellie, was born in Nogales, the oldest of eight sisters, and my father, Bill, was from Tucson, about sixty-five miles away, but he moved to Nogales when he was five. They became high school sweethearts, and afterward, my father went to work for the Southern Pacific Railroad as a cattle clerk while waiting to be drafted into the Army. He eventually did get drafted and was stationed at Camp Roberts in Pasorobles, California, while my mother moved to Oakland, California, and graduated from College of the Holy Name, the same Catholic college my grandmother attended. After graduating, she studied to become a teacher in Oakland. My father, meanwhile, was sent to officer's training school in Georgia. While waiting to be shipped out following his graduation, he rendezvoused with my mother in Nogales and they were married, after which, they didn't see each other for two years.

When my father got out of the Army, he enrolled at the University of California at Berkeley, while my mother taught school in Oakland. During that time, they had their first child, Adrienne, whom we called Penny. They then moved back to Nogales.

My mother's maiden name is Joffroy. Her grandfather, who worked for the United Sugar Company, was part French. Her mother was a Spaniard from Seville who met my grandfather during the Mexican Revolution. She had come to the United States during the revolution to flee Pancho Villa, who was persecuting the Spaniards living in Mexico and taking away their land grants. My mother's father opened the first wholesale bakery in Mexico.

In 1917, my grandfather was waiting to be drafted and decided to go to Mexico by train to take care of some business. He was told not to go because the Yaquis Indians were revolting against the Mexican government, which had been selling the Yaquis' wives as servants. A friend of his was sending his daughter to Mexico at the same time, and asked my grandfather to take care of her. They were sitting in the train's observation car when they saw the Yaquis, all dressed in blue, coming over the hill. He told the girl to do whatever they wanted her to, no matter what. But when she refused to take off her clothes as they ordered, they killed her. The Yaquis then shot my grandfather in the leg and chest. Luckily, he had put his hand in front of him, and the bullet took off three of his fingers. They removed all his clothes and threw him off the train. They started kicking him, but he pretended he was dead. It turned out he was one of only a few survivors. The conductor hid in an ice chest, but they found him and stuck an ice pick in his heart. It was a real bloodbath. My grandfather eventually was found, and after being returned to Nogales, he was sent to New York to recover from his injuries. He later met my grandmother and after they were married, they had to live in Mexico because my grandfather worked there — it was a law at that time. My grandmother hated living in Mexico; eventually they returned to the United States, settling in Nogales, Arizona.

My grandmother on my father's side was part Spanish and part Anglo-Saxon. She married Pierre Eugene Baffert, who was part Spanish and part French. The name Baffert actually is pronounced *Baffeer*. Even with all the mixture of nationalities, my family is very much a part of Americana. My great-great-grandfather on my father's side traveled the Oregon Trail on a wagon train.

I was born on January 13, 1953, and named after my grandmother's brother, who won two Purple Hearts in World War I. He had been returning home after being gassed by mustard when his ship was torpedoed one hundred and twenty miles out of Liverpool. The name of the ship was *Carpathia*, the same ship that had rescued the survivors from the *Titanic*. Two months after I was born, my parents bought a ranch about four miles outside of Nogales. Back then, that was the middle of nowhere. It was pretty desolate out there and we were totally isolated, with no neighbors within miles.

The area was high desert, about 4,000 feet above sea level and located on top of a valley, so it got pretty cold in the winter. We had hills behind the house and there were acres of fields all around. My father had always loved horses, and he decided he wanted a ranch of his own, so he could have a place to raise them. He brought my mother out to see the house. It was built in 1902, and was made mostly of mud adobe. When they got out there, it was locked, so my mother could only look through the window. She took one look at what she thought were hardwood floors and fell in love with it. But as it turned out, it was only linoleum that looked like hardwood. The floors, in actuality, were rotted, and they had to rip them all up.

The house didn't even have electricity, and the only light they had was provided by gas lanterns. They had to wire the whole house and install gas pipes in the attic. My mother wound up remodeling the entire house, and as each kid was born, they kept extending it. It turned out to be a great house, with a huge living room and dining room. Bill and I shared one room, and Penny and Norie shared another. P. A. and Dee Dee were only seventeen months apart, and they shared a room when they were younger. After Dee Dee, my mother thought her child-bearing days were behind her, but seven years later, Gamble was born. They had to figure out where to put him, so they added another bedroom.

In addition to having a few horses, we had a good-sized herd of cattle, mainly Aberdeen Angus show cattle, which we bred to sell.

Being isolated and having no television, we came to depend on each other for entertainment, which made us a very close-knit family. The way the house was situated, with a big hill behind it, we couldn't get any reception, regardless of where we put the antenna. We finally found a spot out in the front field where we could get reception, but the cattle would keep knocking it down. We put a fence around it, but somehow they still managed to knock it down. My parents finally said forget it, and we just went without television for many years.

When I was four, I went through my Aunt Ludie days. Aunt Ludie was my mother's sister. She had been teaching school in San Francisco, then decided to join the Army as a teacher. While she was going through the red tape and waiting for her overseas assignment, she went to Nogales, Mexico, and stayed with my grandmother and grandfather. As it turned out, it was almost a year before she got her assignment, and during that time she came to visit us and immediately fell in love with me. She loved me with a passion. It wasn't anything I did or said; I guess I was just irresistible, even then.

Ludie brought me to stay with my grandparents, who also were crazy about me, and they spoiled me rotten. My grandfather was a very finicky eater, and insisted on having the best of everything. It didn't take me long to adapt that same philosophy. If my grandfather and I ate ice cream, for example, it had to be homemade. With my grandfather being part French, I'd wind up trying delicacies like escargot, and other things most four-year-olds normally don't eat.

While in Nogales, Ludie taught a class called 1-C, for kids who were unfamiliar with the English language. Once they learned it, they went on to first grade. Ludie would take me to school with her, and by the end of the year, I had learned how to read. By the time I got to first grade I was bored to tears. My mother always regretted not having me skip first grade.

That whole school year, I would go back and forth to stay with Aunt Ludie, who would take me on trips, and being proper and a neat freak, would dress me up and make me wash my hands constantly. Whenever I came home, I'd be all dressed up in a bow tie, with my shirt buttons buttoned all the way to the top, and would sit at the dinner table and criticize everyone's table manners, making sure their napkins were in their lap. And being around Aunt Ludie all the time, I would correct everyone's grammar. It would drive my brothers and sisters crazy. Everyone on the ranch was dressed in Levis, and here came this Little Lord Fauntleroy. My father would say to my mother, "What's the matter with your sister? She's going to make a sissy out of the kid." Luckily, Aunt Ludie finally received her assignment to teach school in Spain and I came home and rejoined reality.

My mother was a teacher in Nogales, and eventually became principal. She was a big softie. She'd yell at us all the time, and although we'd never listen to her, we did respect her. She was a great mother. If one of us got sick, she'd stay up with us all night by our bedside. My father was a workaholic. The poor guy would work all day, and was always busy with something. When we were kids, every year at the end of July, he would throw all of us in the station wagon and drive to Mission Beach near San Diego, hauling our boat behind us. He'd just pack the suitcases, put the seats down and lay us down with pillows and blankets and head off. We looked like the *Griswolds* going to California. I remember, we'd always overheat going over the Jacumba Mountains. Once we got to Mission Beach, my father would get us set up in an apartment, get the boat out on the water, then drive back to Nogales to work. Four weeks later, he'd come back to pick us up.

Once in a while we'd hit Disneyland, and one time, I remember heading up there on the highway and coming to this beach that had a statue of a guy with a surfboard. I asked where we were, and my father said Huntington Beach. This is where all the famous surfers would hang out. I remember saying, "Man, oh man, would I love to live here." And that's where I wound up living when I moved to California, and where I still live. I had forgotten all about that incident until after I moved there. That's what I mean about fate.

The older we got, the closer we all became, because we would spend so much time together. We'd get in all kinds of fights. Bill was the oldest brother and he'd bully us all around, but P. A. and I would fight all the time. We'd beat the hell out of each other. But one rule we had was that you could hit anywhere except the face. The toughest of all of us was Norie. When she got mad and curled her tongue, she'd come after you, and you'd better get the hell out of there.

One day, when I was about ten or eleven, I was coming back from school with my cousin John Baffert, who was also my best friend. He was older and bigger than I was, and we got into a fight after getting off the bus. He lived across the road from us, and we went over to his house to fight. I put my fists up and he jabs me right in the nose and it starts bleeding. My nose would bleed over the slightest thing. Meanwhile, Norie is watching all this. She drops her books, curls her tongue, and jumps on top of John and throws him to the ground. And I'm telling you, she just starts beating the crap out of him. She'd get into fights in high school all the time.

We didn't even have a movie house in Nogales. There had been one, but they tore it down and turned it into a dress shop. There was a drive-in, and that was about the only place to go on weekends. It was located right next to a swamp, and there were tons of mosquitoes, so everyone would have to put oil all over their bodies. But I couldn't stand having that stuff on me, so I'd get bitten everywhere. My mother would make us get in our pajamas before we went, because we used to fall asleep during the movie, and this way they could just dump us in bed when we got home. Here I am eleven years old, and I'd go get a Coke during intermission, and all my friends would see me in my goddamn pajamas.

I learned to speak Spanish early because we always had two Mexican housekeepers, and if you wanted something, you had to be able to speak Spanish. Pretty soon, I could speak it fluently.

I had already become hooked on horses. Each day, I'd ride the bus home from school, and I couldn't wait to get back and saddle up my horse. I was a member of the 4-H Club and had my own steer and lambs. I couldn't stand those lambs. They were stinkin' sonofaguns. I had this one lamb who was reserve champion, and one year in Sonoita, Arizona, he got pneumonia on me at the show. He was getting sicker and sicker and was panting away. We worked on him all night. Then this one big ol' cowboy came over and said to my father, "Well, Bill, a sick lamb is a dead lamb." I'll never forget that guy saying that. Sure enough, that poor little lamb died that night. I cried all night.

One year, my father decided to go out and buy a dozen baby chicks, just to have eggs at the house. Then he bought fifty more — half chickens and half roosters. Then, as he started to get more, he built chicken houses. It was difficult getting fresh eggs back then. There were no chickens in Arizona, and the eggs would have to come all the way from Kansas. By the time they got to Arizona they were old and smelled awful. So, people would come around wanting to buy eggs from my father.

He kept on expanding, and eventually had almost 20,000 chickens, all in individual cages. As it turned out, the guy who used to sell and deliver the eggs for us quit and became the janitor at my mother's school. There was no one to deliver the eggs, so I volunteered to do it during high school. We produced twenty-five cases of eggs a day, and would sell them for ten dollars a case. Two hundred and fifty dollars a day was big money in those days. I'd come home from school, load the eggs on the back of our old pick-up, and go out and sell them wholesale to the big store owners and make my own deals.

I'd decide to have a big sale and sell them for thirty-nine cents a dozen. My father would scream, "Thirty-nine cents a dozen? You're crazy." But I'd tell him we had to move them. They're not like wine. They don't improve with age. It was through the chickens that I learned how to relate to people and make good business deals. I kept helping my father in the egg business. I would go to the stores, restaurants, and hotels and ask if they needed eggs. Then after I made the deal, I would deliver them. There was one cook at the El Dorado Hotel, who knew I loved sweets, and every time I'd come with a delivery he'd make me a cream pie. Everyone would tell me what a great salesman I was. I guess that's how I learned people skills.

I remember some of the wild egg fights we used to have. My brothers and sisters would go down and pick up all the eggs and put them in cardboard filler flats. My parents normally would hire people to do it, like cowboys and ranch hands. But sometimes, if they were out drinking on a Saturday night, they wouldn't show up Sunday morning, and we all had to go out and do it. It was a horrible job. The hen houses were really long, with rows and rows of cages. The cages were slanted, so the eggs would roll down. As soon as you'd walk in there, the chickens would go nuts, cackling and flapping their wings, and their dusty feed would fly all over us. We'd come out with all that dust on our faces and in our hair. But we'd go in there and collect the eggs.

Then one day, things got really out of hand, and we had this incredible egg fight. We had all our friends out and just unloaded. The hen houses were set against an embankment of red earth. It started out with one of us saying, "Look how far I can throw this." Before we knew it, we were throwing hundreds of eggs all over the place. Then we started throwing the eggs at each other. My father was furious. Eventually, when I went off to college, my father closed down the egg business. To this day, I won't eat eggs.

My father was always very handy, and so were Bill, P. A., and Gamble. My father could fix anything and did all the electricity in the house. I can't recall us ever calling a plumber. My brothers were able to pick it up, but I was a lazy sonofagun. I just didn't want to learn. I was also Mr. Clean. I didn't want to get dirty. It must have been from my Aunt Ludie days. We'd go to brand the cattle, and my father would say, "Come on, get in there and get dirty." But I couldn't stand it. The cattle were dirty and dusty and I didn't want to have anything to do with that.

I became closest to P. A. Bill was older, and when he got in high school, he'd go across the border and get drunk every night. My mother would not go to sleep until every one of us was home. She'd sit there on the couch with the light on, reading a book and smoking a cigarette until everybody came in. My sister Penny was the wild one and she'd put my mother through hell.

I started getting on horses when I was five or six. I just loved being on them. I was the only one of my brothers and sisters who really loved the horses and working with them. Norie loved horses, but in a romantic and passionate way. She'd ride a lot and would sing to them, but once she started high school, she found other interests.

When I was about ten or eleven, I had this friend named Rickie Cepeda whose family had a big cattle ranch in Mexico. One time, he asked me if I wanted to go with them on a cattle drive. We flew down there in a private plane, and took 3,000 head of cattle on a three-day drive on horseback. For a hundred miles, I rode this big, ol' Mexican horse. It was like the movie *City Slickers*. We slept in sleeping bags and lived on canned tuna fish and tortillas. I'd ride on point, leading the drive, and we'd get to a water hole and stop to fill up our canteens. I remember there was all this shit in the water, and we had to drink first before the cattle, because once the cattle drank, the water would get all murky. We drove the herd from the ranch to Sasabe, Arizona, going right through the middle of town. I mean, I was a cowboy dude. I really learned how to ride on that drive. The Mexican cowboys were great horsemen, and they would show me how to go after the cattle and brush down the horse.

But there was still that pansy in me. I had to poop while I was out there, but I didn't want to poop in the middle of nowhere, and when I asked the Mexican guys what they used to wipe themselves, they said they used rocks. So I held it in for three days.

After that, I started riding one of our horses named Baffert's

Heller. What a beautiful horse he was. Years later, when I was train-ing horses, I used him as my pony. My father got started with race-horses when I was about ten, buying this Quarter Horse mare, and my uncle, F. J. Baffert, had some Quarter Horse mares of his own. He and my dad bought a few horses together, and they decided to put one of them in training, and that was Baffert's Heller. He won a cou-ple of races, and I remember going with him one time to Rillito Downs and he didn't run very well. I started going to the track with my father, and my job was to pack the binoculars for him.

The guy who got my father started in the racehorse business was Blain Lewis, from Patagonia. He raised Quarter Horses, and that's who they bought the mares from. He'd break our horses and get them ready for us. He had a system where he wouldn't put a water bucket in a horse's stall. They only drank water twice a day — when they were walked by hand after exercising, and when they walked in the afternoon. He said it kept them tighter.

When Baffert's Heller quit running, my father sent him to someone to make a riding horse out of him. I always told my dad I wanted to ride Baffert's Heller. So when we got him back, I'd saddle him up and ride him. I was used to riding these big, ugly, goofy-look-ing Mexican horses, and when Baffert's Heller showed up, man, I was in awe of him. He was so beautiful. When I first started to sad-dle him up, he could sense I was afraid of him and he'd try to buck me off. It took me about a year to master that sonofagun.

Although I had no thoughts of being a jockey at that point, I do remember when I was a little kid, I'd come home from school and run around the house with a fly swatter, pretending it was a whip.

My father then bought two fillies and named them Baffert's Gypsy and Baffert's Belle — he put Baffert in front of all the horses' names. He sent Baffert's Belle to a trainer who ran her in the Futurity

Trials at Prescott Downs. She qualified for the Futurity, and we needed a rider for her. The purse was only about ten thousand dollars.
The trainer called up my father and said he's got a real good jockey
coming in to ride her. My father asked what his name was, and the
trainer said Ray York. Neither one of us had ever heard of him. The
trainer said he won the Kentucky Derby in 1954 aboard Determine.
And I'll never forget my father saying, "Well, what the hell happened to him? What's he doing coming to Prescott Downs?" He
rode her well, finishing third. Years later, they had that Rocking
Chair Derby at Del Mar for the old-time riders, where you drew for
a rider. I put a horse in there, and guess who I drew? Ray York. And
the horse won. I said to him, "Man, I haven't seen you since I was a
little kid at Prescott Downs."

Is it a small world or what? That's what I mean about things happening to me. Things happen for a reason. Because of that, I just get a
horse ready for a race the best way I can and let fate take over. If I'm
supposed to win, I'm going to win it. If I'm supposed to have bad luck,
I'm going to have bad luck. I really believe that's the way it works.

SHORT IN THE SADDLE

"When Bobby was ten years old he was already riding the horses. He was a natural horseman, and even when he was a kid he could pick out a good horse. At twelve and thirteen, he already had the ability to tell me right away if a horse was good or not. He had great balance and broke all the horses at the ranch. You'd look at this skinny kid and would never think he'd ever be able to handle these kind of horses, but he broke every-thing — yearlings and two-year-olds — and he'd gallop them. Those same attributes he had as a kid, he uses now." — *Bill Baffert Sr.*

I was in junior high school, but racehorses were now a major part of my life. We had a few decent horses, and I was about to start riding competitively. I soon would discover one of the most exhilarating feelings in the world. It was quite an experience for an eleven-year-old.

Baffert's Gypsy was a pretty good little mare, running on the Arizona fair circuit, winning a few trials. We had her with trainer Kenny Dunlap. My dad brought her home and decided he could cut out a little strip on the ranch and train the horses ourselves. And he told me I could be the exercise boy. We went to Sonoita, and I remember, there was this guy named Charles McNulty who trained and made tack on the side. McNulty looked like that grizzled old guy who drove the wagon and got killed by the Indians in *Dances With Wolves*. He was just a scruffy little guy, and he made us our first exer-

62

cise saddle. That was one uncomfortable sonofagun. It was so awkward, and I had to keep practicing with it on Baffert's Heller.

We brought Baffert's Heller to Sonoita, and I put the exercise saddle on. I took him on the track and jacked the stirrups up, and I think I fell off three times. Every time he moved, the saddle fell off. When I got back to the ranch, I lowered the stirrups, and little by little I got used to it. I would also tie the saddle straps and put my feet in between whenever I went out to bring in the cows. I did that for six months, and finally, I told my father the saddle sucked, and we went out and got another one in Ruidoso, New Mexico.

I had started exercising Baffert's Gypsy, and would get on her each day before leaving for school. She was so much fun to ride. Every time I rode her she'd tell me when she had had enough. We sent her to Ruidoso Downs for a race and she ran horribly. While we were there, we went to the Johnny Bean tack shop and bought what they called a Bob Ross exercise saddle. It was expensive and very cushiony. In fact, everybody uses them now. I still use that same saddle at Santa Anita.

By this time, I'm starting to think a little about being a jockey. We'd bring Baffert's Gypsy to the different fairs every weekend. My dad would be the trainer and I'd be the groom and lead her up there. I'd hold her while my dad put the saddle on. She was a pretty good filly and she won a few races, but we didn't know what the hell we were doing.

My father liked to drink a lot of beer, and he'd have friends come over and talk about horses and breeding. He liked to mix up his own liniments, using witch hazel, Absorbine, and rubbing alcohol. Every night, I'd have to sit there and rub the horses' legs for three hours while he was drinking beer with his buddies. My mother would wait with dinner, but the Chief, which is what we called my father, would never go up to the house because he knew my mom would get mad at him for drinking beer. So that's why I had to sit there for three hours rubbing the horses' legs. She'd get furious with him, and finally, she'd come down to the barn and get after him to come in.

My brother Bill, meanwhile, was really good at showing the steers, but he really wasn't into the horses, although he eventually wound up training for a while. P. A. would help out a little bit, but he'd quit all the time. You couldn't get him mad. The minute he got mad he'd quit.

One time, Bill won a trip to Kentucky with the 4-H Club and brought back pictures of great stallions like Nashua. I was really impressed. I couldn't believe he got to see all these great horses. Even though we were dealing with Quarter Horses, my dad started ordering *The Blood-Horse* magazine, so we knew all the great Thoroughbreds and all the top trainers. He even bought Preston Burch's book on how to train Thoroughbreds, and I read that, so I had a pretty good idea what was going on.

By the time I was a freshman in high school I had gotten pretty good at riding and breezing the horses. I was little, and my father would bring me to these match races, for hundred-dollar pots. Of course, the betting there was illegal. It was Mexican-style racing, which was sitting on the horse bareback, putting the overgirth over the rider's thighs and ankles, then putting a golf ball in each front pocket to keep the overgirth from slipping to the knees. You're on there; you can't fall off. And the golf balls would prevent the girth from slipping. The only bad thing was that if the horse flipped in the gate or bolted or broke down, you were in big trouble.

So I started riding in these match races, and because I was so little it was easy to just haul ass. My dad would pick me up from school and bring my helmet, my boots, and my whip, then take me straight to the match races. Obviously we didn't tell my mother about it. She didn't want me doing this because it was too dangerous. So my dad and I lived a very secretive life. We were always in a stealth mode, him with his beer and me with my riding. We had a deal. I'd never say anything about him drinking beer and he'd never say anything about me being a jockey. That's why we became so close. When we'd get home, my mother would ask me, "Has your father been drinking?" And I'd say, "No, he hasn't had a drink all day." And every time she'd ask my father if I'd been riding, he'd say, "Of course not."

My father was so funny with his beer drinking. He'd have us trained how to throw the empty cans out the car window so no state trooper could spot it. He'd always say, "You always hold the can down and keep your arm down to the side of the car when you release it. When I give you the signal, you just toss it straight down. You don't want to throw it, because then they can see the arc." He had it down to a science. So he'd be sitting there, and I'm holding the can out the window, and he'd go, "Okay, now." I'm telling you, the Chief had it down to perfection.

One day, my father picked me up from school, and I rode this Thoroughbred in a match race and he won. The guy paid me fifty bucks, and when you're a freshman in high school, that's a lot of money, especially back in the '60s. Now, I had the fever. I went back and won another one and I got a hundred bucks. I had the dough coming in now. I went up to Tucson and bought myself some nice bell-bottom pants and other clothes.

By the following year, I was doing pretty good and riding more and more. One day, we went up to Tubac, Arizona, for a big match race. My uncle went with us. He had a horse of his own and he'd come across the street and use our track. One day, we had a match race between his horse and my dad's horse. His horse won and my dad got mad and locked the gate and wouldn't let him use our track anymore.

So now, the three of us drive up to Tubac for this match race, and I'm in the gate waiting to break. I didn't know it at the time, but the connections of the other horse had been stiffing him and were setting up a big betting score in this race. The way the place was situated, all the cars were parked on a road alongside the track. There were easily five hundred cars parked there. It was a big occasion. They had a mariachi band and lots of food. It was like a big picnic. Of course, it was all illegal gambling, but nobody knew what was going on there.

We break from the gate, and my horse just fires away from there. But this other horse goes "whoosh" and throws about two lengths on me, and we're only going about three hundred yards. All of a sudden, the other horse bolts and goes off the track and behind the cars and into the crowd. And with all this, the other jock is still riding him. He's going in between the cars. I don't know what the hell is going on, so I just keep riding my horse. Then I look up and everybody is standing on the track in front of me. I start yelling and they open up and I get through and win the race. The other horse, meanwhile, winds up in the goddamn trees.

Then, the minute I stand up on my horse, the stirrup breaks. It was a brand new stirrup. Someone had cut it in half, but it didn't break until after the race. I'm going, "Sonofabitch, what the hell did I get myself into?" After the race, everyone is paying off, and this one guy is really pissed off. There was a lot of big money lost on the race. I come back and I show everyone the stirrup, and they're going, "Hey, look at this shit. What's goin' on here?" So they pay me two hundred bucks. That was my take on the deal.

Some of the judges then start talking about running the race over, and the people who bet on my horse are going "Bullshit, man." My dad had bet five hundred bucks on my horse and he's getting all excited. Before the race, he mentioned to a friend that he bet the horse, and the guy tells him, "Oh man, Bill, you should have told me first. There's a fix in on the other horse." After the race, the guy he bet with couldn't pay him all the money and gave him a lasso rope to make up the difference.

Meanwhile, there's this one big guy who is really upset, and all of a sudden a fistfight breaks out, and the big guy starts smacking the hell out of these two younger guys. One of them runs off, and just then, my uncle yells out, "Hit the ground." This guy is back with a rifle and starts shooting up the place, trying to smoke this guy who just whacked him. Now there are fights breaking out all over and everyone is jumping in their cars and hauling ass out of there. It was total chaos.

We're driving down the road alongside the track and heading for the gate, and the dust being kicked up from all the cars is horrendous. You can't see anything. We look up and there's this one drunk guy in a station wagon, and he goes blowing by us on the racetrack. I tell my father, "If he stays on the track he's gonna run right into the starting gate." Just then, I hear this crash. The guy is leaning forward on the horn and he's knocked unconscious. The windshield is busted and his face is all bloody. I'm telling you, it was unbelievable — a hell of an experience for a high school sophomore.

As we're driving home, my dad tells my uncle, "We can't come back here anymore. I can't bring Bobby here. If his mother finds out what the hell went on today, she won't let me take him anywhere ever again." So we had to keep it all very quiet.

I kept riding in match races, but in much safer places. We started training more horses, and when I turned sixteen, I started thinking seriously about being a jockey. But if you were under the age of seventeen you had to have both parents' signatures, and there was no way I was going to get my mother to sign, so I couldn't get my license. Finally, I turned seventeen, and my father and I went out and bought jockey pants and a saddle, and had silks made up. But my feet were so big I had trouble finding jockey boots and had to have them made specially for me. Every night, late at night, I'd lock the door to my room, put on my jockey outfit and get in front of the mirror and pretend like I was riding.

Around this time, my hair started to turn gray, and I'd pull out all the gray ones. But as it got grayer, I stopped fighting it. By the age of thirty, my hair would be completely white, something I inherited from my grandfather on my mother's side.

I was on summer vacation, and I had to ride in three races in order to get my license. I also had to work a horse out of the gate in front of the stewards at Sonoita. I worked the horse fine, and now I had to find three races to ride. There was this one little Thoroughbred I had been riding in match races who was in at Sonoita and they decided to put me on him. I had only been riding him in match races going three hundred and four hundred yards.

Of course, my mother still doesn't know anything about this. So now I have the mount on this horse. It's 10 o'clock in the morning and all my chores are finished. I get all my gear, which I kept hidden in my room, and go take a shower. Just then, the phone rings and it's this friend of my mother's named Nora Pickerall. She was very horse oriented. She had jumpers of her own and followed racing very closely. She says to my mother, "Ellie, I just want to wish Bobby good luck today."

"What do you mean?" my mother says. And Nora tells her, "I see in the entries he's riding a horse at Sonoita today. It's right there — R. Baffert. Who else can it be?" My mother is adamant. "No, he's

not," she insists. "Nora, he is not a jockey. He just rides the cow horses. There is no way he's riding in a race."

I get out of the shower and my mother asks me, "Are you riding a horse today as a jockey?" I'm totally speechless and start bab-
bling, "Uh, well, what do you mean? No, you know, well, we are
going to the races." My mother shoots right back, "What are you
going to do there?" I tell her we're just going to watch the races. So
she tells me about Nora Pickerall's phone call. She goes over and
picks up the paper and finds the entries herself. I finally tell her that
we didn't want to say anything because we knew she'd get nervous
and we didn't want her to worry.

Well, I'm telling you, she was furious. Then she starts crying and
telling me how dangerous it is. I try to reassure her, explaining that
I've ridden this horse before and I know him really well. I tell her that
I've ridden in all these match races and won a lot of them. And she
just stops me in my tracks. "You've done what?" she screams.

During all this, my father is down by the barn getting ready and
he has no idea what's going on. When I see him, I tell him, "We're
busted. Nora Pickerall called and told Mom I was riding today." He
gets to the house, and my mom starts chewing him out big-time and
calling us liars and sneaks. Then, she starts pleading with me not to
go. But I tell her, "Mom, I have to go." And I head out of there.

We drive to Sonoita and I go straight to the jocks' room. What
a grungy, low-class crew. I was told beforehand not to take any
money or valuables in there, because they'll fleece you while you're
out there riding. I had about twenty bucks in my pocket, and when
I got back it was gone. They were just a degenerate bunch of jocks
who couldn't make it anywhere else.

While I'm getting dressed, I'm a nervous sonofagun. I come out
and get on the horse and I can't believe it. I'm actually riding in a

real race. I'm in the gate and I'm holding on to the horse's mane, and the gates fly open. I'll never forget it. I felt like I was in this dream. I had been used to riding in three-hundred-yard Quarter Horse match races, and now I'm on this Thoroughbred going five furlongs at a real racetrack. I get squeezed back, and the others start getting away from me. I'm near the back of the pack and I'm getting pelted with rocks and dirt. All the shit from the track is just showering down on me. I had never experienced that before. I just keep taking him farther back until the rocks are hitting me lower down.

I'm just sitting on him and I'm getting real tired. My butt is hitting the saddle and I'm looking like a sack of shit. Finally, I finish the race. I run dead last and come back and tell everyone, "Man, I don't think I did very well out there." The trainer says, "You've ridden that horse better than that. Your goddamn butt was hitting the back of the horse. What the hell happened?"

When I got home, my mother was waiting for us, and she was a nervous wreck. She never really did accept me being a jockey, but she knew it was something I desperately wanted and was determined to do.

I still had two more races to ride, so we went to Yuma, where we were going to run this little filly of ours named Baffert's Doll. This time, Bill came with us, and we all headed off in our pick-up truck with a shell camper on it, hauling the horse behind us. They didn't have stalls at the track; they just had corrals for the horses. I was starting to come down with the flu or something, and the three of us slept in the back of the goddamn truck with my dad and Bill drinking beer all night. It was like a camping trip.

The next day, Baffert's Doll is sick as a dog with a hundred-and-three-degree fever. So now she's sick and I'm sick. We can't run her, so I go to the jocks' room and get another mount. I open up my bag and I realize I forgot to bring my helmet and my whip. I wind up borrowing a helmet, which was too big for me, and borrowing a whip. I get on this horse, and he's dead lame. He's got bandages on all fours. I go behind the gate, no pony or nothing, and this horse literally is limping. The vet comes over and says, "Hey jock, that horse feel okay to you? We checked him out, but you still want to ride him like that?" Well, I needed my three mounts, so I say, "Yeah, he's okay."

This horse was like 80-1 or 90-1. He hadn't done shit. We leave the gate and I keep him on the outside all the way just in case he broke down, and we run fourth. Now I've got two mounts out of the way. We decide to take a few horses up to Prescott Downs, including Baffert's Doll, and stay with some friends of ours in a log cabin.

The day after we arrived, I agreed to breeze a filly, who was owned by the friends we were staying with. While I was working her, the damn cinch broke. They had gotten this saddle in Mexico, and apparently, the cinch had been put on with little nails instead of being sewn on. The nails wound up falling out, causing the saddle to slip. Meanwhile, this filly is hauling ass and I'm smokin' down the track, and the next thing I know, my left foot is on top of the horse's withers. She goes around the turn and I just fly off. When I hit the ground, I hit it with my elbow, jamming it into my kidney. Man, that hurt. It knocked the air right out of me. My side was bruised pretty badly and was sore as hell afterward. That night, when I went to urinate, I urinated blood. But I didn't tell anybody. I figured I just jostled myself up a little.

While I was at Prescott, I had met this old guy and we hit it off pretty good. We'd sit there just shootin' the shit and he really took a liking to me.

The next day, we take Baffert's Doll and haul her up to Flagstaff to run in a race. I get her in the gate, and she rears up and throws me up against the back of the gate, and I hit myself in the same spot. It was already pretty sore, and now it's really smartin'. Anyway, we break and the filly doesn't run a lick. She winds up fourth or fifth. So now I've got my three mounts and I've got my license. I come back to the jocks' room and this guy comes over to me and tells me, "Hey Bob, one of the jocks didn't show up to ride his horse in the next race and the trainer wants you to ride him." The horse is named Sizzling Snark, and I look up and see that he's one of the favorites. I say, "Why the hell does he want me? He's got one of the favorites and I haven't done shit." He said all he knew was that he insisted on using me.

I go out there to meet this guy, and he's the old man I had been talking to at Prescott. Meanwhile, all the other jocks are going, "Hey, if he doesn't want to ride him, I'll ride him." I'm all excited and I go over to my dad and tell him I've got a live mount. We go to the gate, and I go to grab a hold of the horse's mane, which Quarter Horse jockeys often do, and I notice it was completely rubbed out. All he had left were three little strands of hair. All I'm thinking is, "How am I going to break? I have nothing to hold on to." I was really worried.

The gates open, and I'm trying to hold on to something. He breaks like a shot, and he's running right along on the lead and I'm in shock. I can't believe I'm on the lead. Then this other horse, breaking from the one hole, starts drifting all the way out toward me. And his jock is hitting him on the side of the neck and head. I see him coming and I'm thinking, "Holy shit, this horse is going to run right into me." I start whipping my horse, and just like that he starts leaving him. I look around and there is nothing next to me. I'm coming to the wire and I start flagging. When I hit that wire, I'm telling you, it was like winning the Kentucky Derby. I can still remember pulling up and yelling and whooping. You'd have thought I had just won the greatest race in the world. What a great feeling. I'll never forget it.

I come back waving my stick, and my dad's there and P. A.'s there. People are taking pictures of me in the winner's circle. Everyone is congratulating me on my first win. It was just unbeliev-able. I thank the old man and tell him how much this means to me. I go back to the jocks' room and take off my colors, and I notice it's real quiet. All of a sudden, somebody grabs me from behind. All I'm thinking is that these guys are pissed that I won this race and they're going to beat the crap out of me. They all grab me and throw me to the floor. Two guys hold my legs and someone starts undoing my pants and pulling them down. I'm starting to think about these sto-ries you hear in prisons. What the hell are they going to do to me?

Then one guy comes over with a bottle of shoeshine polish and throws it on my privates. And that shit starts stinging me like you wouldn't believe. I ran to the shower, and the cold water made it worse. It actually caused blisters down there, not to mention ruining my pants. Once they threw that stuff on me I realized it was just an initiation and I relaxed a little. But, man, that scared me.

We went back to the hotel and I called the ranch to tell my mother and everyone I won my first race. But I couldn't get through. The phone was dead. I called my uncle, and he told me they had smelled smoke in the house and discovered the attic was on fire. My grandmother was there and she called the fire department. Luckily, they got there quickly and put it out, but it burned the whole top of the attic. When I called, they were still in the process of putting out the fire, and I'm telling you, talk about putting a damper on some-thing. Here I had just won my first race and I couldn't fully enjoy it.

We left early the next morning and my dad was really bummed out. There was all this water damage and the attic was gone. We got back, and the house actually looked pretty good, except for the hole in the attic. The firemen had gone up there and chopped it all up and did some serious damage. You could still smell smoke, and all the carpets in the living room were ruined. My mother lives for her house, and she was really upset.

A week later, we were out in the field with the cattle and we were getting these heifers in. Bill and I had to take a leak. So we're in the field standing next to each other talking, and Bill goes, "Oh my God." I look down and I'm urinating blood again. I told him about falling off this horse and hurting my kidney. Bill went and told my dad and he took me down to this clinic. They took tests and told me I either had a bruised kidney or a torn kidney. I had to go up to the medical center in Tucson immediately for more tests. If it was torn, I was going to have to be operated on that night. I mean, they scared the shit out of me.

My mother was at the home of a Methodist minister, taking a counseling course, and she didn't know about any of this. Someone went to pick her up and bring her home, but instead of going home, they drove her to the hospital. She didn't even know where she was going until someone finally told her. As it turned out, it was just a bruised kidney, but I had to spend five days in the hospital without getting out of bed. When my mom showed up at the hospital, she threw a fit. "I told you," she said. "You disobeyed me. You're not supposed to be a jockey. I want you to quit right now. This is it." I told her it was a freak thing and that I'd be all right.

All she kept saying was, "You don't know what you've put me through." And she was right about that. I did put her through hell with this jockey deal. They told me to take it easy for a month, which I did. But after that I started back again. I respected my mom, but I wanted to ride more than anything.

74

SUBSTANTIVE YEARS

"I met Bob at the University of Arizona and he was the same jokester and prankster in college that he is today. He was like Eddie Haskell from the "Leave it to Beaver" show. He enjoyed a good laugh more than any-thing, and we had some fun times together. We sat next to each other in Agricultural school, and it didn't take us long to start talking horses. If there's one thing I remember about him even then it's that he was an astute observer. He lets you think things are just passing over him, but the guy takes in an awful lot. You don't get to where he has gotten by just slapping everybody on the back and laughing all the time. He has sensory ears and takes in a lot of little things. You may say something to him and feel noth-ing was made of it, but a year later, he'll remember what you said and bring it up to you. He does that with horses and people. One thing about Bob as a horseman, he knows what he wants and he knows what works."

— *Jonabell Farm president Jimmy Bell*

When I was a sophomore in high school, I left the horses for a while and went through my drug stage. It was the hippie generation, and it was cool to smoke a little bit of weed. I really didn't like it, though. I always liked to be in control. But I got involved with these guys and just wanted to be cool. I would leave the house in jeans, but when I got to school I changed into these hip-hugger bellbottoms and flowered shirts and moc-casins. I would wear that during the day, like Mr. Cool. When I'd leave, I changed back into my jeans to go home. I was living two separate lives.

Then we started trying designer drugs like LSD and every type of acid imaginable. Every Friday night, there was a football game and a dance afterward. We would all synchronize our watches. The game would start at seven, and that's when we'd start dropping acid. By the time the game was over and we headed for the dance, we were totally zoned out. The head guy in our group was the star football player, whom Noree went out with. He was the main man, the school hero. He was the first person who turned me on to weed. He took me in his car and we went cruising. He showed me how to do it, and the first time I took a deep breath I passed out.

I remember one night I came home, and my mother was waiting up for me. They had a thing in school at the time where they'd show parents how to check if their kids were doing drugs. I came home and I was completely wiped out. I had dropped some orange acid and was banging on the old pipe all night. I was ripped. Whenever I drove back to the ranch I had everything worked out. When you're stoned, you can be going thirty miles an hour, but you feel like you're going sixty. Just in case I got screwed up, I had the highway marker lined up with these buildings and I knew when to hit the blinker and make a right-hand turn into the ranch.

When you're messed up like that, it's hard to find the doorknob of the house in the dark. This one night, I fumbled for a while and finally got the door open. All of a sudden, the light goes on and my mother is standing there. "Come here," she says. "Let me see you. I can tell if you're on drugs or not." When you smoke dope, you lick your lips a lot, because they get dry, and I had this big old white ring around my lips. My shirt had all these little holes in it from where the ashes had burned through. I had every sign imaginable. My mother says, "Let me look in your eyes." She looks in my eyes and says, "Okay, I was just checking."

My father was the county supervisor at the time, and he came home one day and told me, "They just showed me a list of the top ten guys in the high school who are doing drugs, and your name was on it. It broke my heart." He said, "I'm not going to ask you if this is true, but remember one thing: I'm a supervisor, and if you get caught, it's going to be very humiliating for me and your mother. I just want you to think about that."

The heat was starting to build up in the town. A few nights later, I'm driving home and I happen to be sober at the time. I get pulled over by the border patrol agents in an unmarked car. They ask to see my license and they look at my eyes and ask me if I'd been drinking or taking drugs. I said no, and they told me it was just a spot check and that I could go. That scared the shit out of me, and it really woke me up. I went back to my friends and told them to count me out. I couldn't do the drugs anymore. They got real pissed off at me because what I was doing wasn't cool. As it turned out, they all wound up going to jail and didn't amount to anything. It was when I got away from the drugs that I really got back into my horses.

The summer after I graduated from high school in 1971, I took this mare named Baffert's Lady to Los Alamitos, and I stayed in an apartment complex near Anaheim with a fellow we knew from Nogales named Manny Molera, who had Quarter Horses. I had ridden a few horses for him on the Arizona fair circuit. He told my dad he'd take care of me and watch over me. We hired a guy named Jim Greenslate and put the horses in his name because I wasn't licensed in California. Jim was a nice old guy, and he had some problems, so we helped him out. Manny did most of the training and I'd help him. I won a race on Baffert's Lady, who became my dad's first winner in California.

I galloped the horses and won a few races, and at the end of the summer I rode a horse for a guy named Jim Monji, who was the private trainer for Dr. Ed Allred, who is now the owner of Los Alamitos. A few days before the end of the meet, he had this horse in named Gaberino, who was a real rogue, ducking and diving every time he ran.

Jim asked me if I wanted to ride the horse and I said sure. I had no fear at all back then. So I ride him and he finishes second. But as I'm pulling up, this horse on the inside of me comes out toward me, and Gaberino just ducks away from him. Just then, I hear the jock behind me, yell, "Hey, hey, hey!" The next thing I know, he clips heels with my horse and goes down. I turn around and see him fall and my heart just drops. I pull up, and all I'm thinking is, "Oh my God, I've hurt somebody."

When I got back, the ambulance was there, and I was feeling awful. If he had gotten hurt real bad, I would have quit riding right then and there. Luckily, he just had a sore collarbone. I apologized to him, and I felt if he wanted to beat the crap out of me, he could, because I deserved it for dropping him.

After the meet ended, I was supposed to go back home and get ready to go to college at the University of Arizona in Tucson. But I called my mom and told her I wasn't going to college that year. I said I could always go to college, but with my weight, I can't be a jockey all my life, so I wanted to continue riding while I could. Well, of course, she was devastated. Again, I heard the same deal. "God, you're killing me. You don't know what you've put me through." My father finally told her, "Don't force him to go to school. If you do, he's only going to flunk out." So she reluctantly gave in.

She had come to see me ride once and she couldn't look. She

had to go behind the building and listen to the call. I remember one time we went to break a horse out of the gate, and we needed somebody to pull the lever, so we asked my mom. I was in the gate and my dad was in the back getting ready to slap the horse out. My dad tells her, "Okay, when we go 'one, two, three,' you pull on the rope and it'll open it up." She pulled on the rope and I left there hollering and screaming. Well, she thought I was screaming because I was falling off, and she starts crying. That's just the way she was. She couldn't take it.

After school, I started looking for a job. The person I really wanted to work for was Wayne Lukas. I was going to call him up to see if I could gallop horses for him, and I'll never forget, I was scared to death. He was the king, and I really liked his style. The first time I ever saw him was in Sonoita, Arizona. When he showed up, he just took over. I mean it was a show. When Wayne rolled into town it was like Barnum and Bailey. He was a showman to the max, and I really liked that. I wrote down everything I wanted to say so I wouldn't forget it. I finally found the nerve to call him, in his hotel, and I think I woke him up.

"Mr. Lukas?" I said. "My name is Bob Baffert, and I'm here in Arizona. I've been riding horses a little and going to school, and I'd love to work for you as a gallop boy and learn." You can't believe how nervous I was. He could have just said, "I have a lot of people already and I don't need you." But he goes, "You know what? I did need a gallop boy and I just hired someone a few days ago. It's too bad, because you would have been perfect for my operation. I'd been looking for someone just like you." He really built me up. When I got off the phone, I felt great, even though I didn't get the job. Whether he really did just hire someone or not, it didn't matter. He left me with this great impression and made me feel good about myself. As it turned out, I don't think I would have lasted too long with Wayne. He just gets up too damn early. It would have been a tough grind and he would have fired my ass in an instant.

The following January, I got a call from Jim Monji, and he tells me he wants me to come ride for him third string and work as a gallop boy. He says to me, "You know, Bob, I'd sure like to have you. You showed a lot of guts riding my horse." All I kept thinking was, "What an opportunity, to go to work for Dr. Allred." So my dad drives me back to Los Alamitos, where I'm to break all of Jim's horses. We get a cot and my dad sets me up in the tack room with my own little dresser and leaves me there.

We would start galloping horses at six in the morning until three in the afternoon. I got on so many horses I had all these blisters on my ass. We stayed there for a month, then laid the horses up at the farm in Atascadero for a week before sending them up to Bay Meadows. It just so happened, my brother Bill was living near Bay Meadows at the time, working for Johnson & Johnson, so I moved in with him and it worked out great.

I galloped horses and rode a few, and Dr. Allred really got to like me. He called me, "The Baffler." He'd tell Jimmy Monji, "I want The Baffler to win a race." Dr. Allred was a big gambler. He was a bettin' sonofagun. One day, he told Jimmy he wanted to run this one horse and drop him from five thousand to sixteen hundred claiming, just so I could win a race. He was a pretty nice horse. I wound up winning the race, and afterward, there were about ten claims in for the horse. He got claimed and went on to win about five in a row after that.

I remember, one day after we went back down to Los Alamitos, word got out that they were going to raid the jocks' room for batteries. You should have seen those jockeys running around there. There was this little lake in the back, and these guys ran out and started throwing all these batteries in the water. After that, they started to police the place pretty well and we never had any problems.

I won a couple of races at Los Alamitos and decided to go back home in the summer. I really hadn't been ready mentally for college. I was still very immature. I even looked five or six years younger than I was. That's one of the reasons I decided to wait a year, and I'm glad I did.

When I did finally start college in Tucson, I had a blast. I joined a fraternity house, which was right across the street from Noree's sorority. We became very close and would help each other out. I met one of her sorority sisters, Alicia Pappas, and we went out for three years. We talked horses and really hit it off. She eventually dropped me like a burnt match and it took me a long time to get over it. I wound up losing ten pounds.

One night, there was this big function, and everybody had a date. Noree didn't want to go out with the guy who asked her, so she told him she already had a date. When all the other guys heard that, no one bothered to ask her, so she wound up with no date at all. As it turned out, I became her date. I picked her up in my car so she could tell everyone, "Hey, my date's here." Noree knew I loved chocolate cake, so she went out and bought one. We went to this park nearby and just sat there eating chocolate cake all night.

Noree was something. I set her up on a blind date one time, and she didn't like the guy at all. He took her to the door, and Noree had had a few drinks. She was nervous that this guy was going to try to kiss her. She reached for the door and it was locked. She started pulling on the door so hard, she pulled it right off its hinges. That was the talk of the school. Afterward, she told me, "Don't you ever set me up with anybody again."

During that freshman year, I galloped horses occasionally in the morning and actually rode in one race. I rode Baffert's Baron and he won. But my weight was killing me, so I stopped riding for the time being.

The following summer, I worked briefly at Los Alamitos for a trainer named Vern Goodman, who wanted me to gallop horses for him and be his assistant. When I got there, I found out that this groom of his had quit the same day I arrived. So not only did I gallop horses, I had to clean a few stalls as well. And I'll tell you, that's a sonofabitch. I also wound up ponying his horses to the gate at night, so it was a full-time deal. While I was there, I met John Bassett, who would become my best friend. John was one wild guy. He was raised in Globe, Arizona, and now lives in Dewey with his family, still training Quarter Horses. He eventually trained some Thoroughbreds, and when I made the switch, John sent me many of my early stakes winners.

John's father, Joe Bassett, was a great horseman and Quarter Horse trainer who taught him everything he knows. I went back home to return to the University of Arizona, and John went back to Arizona to train horses, and we hung out together quite a lot in Tucson.

After John and I got back to Arizona, Bill quit his job with Johnson & Johnson and he came back, and we all lived together in Tucson. I told Bill, "You got to meet this guy. He's a fun guy." We all hit it off and had some wild times together.

There was one time, we were having a Christmas party and Bassett says to me, "Let's streak through the living room." Streaking was really popular at the time. What he wanted to do was streak through the living room and yell, "Remember the Alamo." So, we get undressed and Bassett says, "Okay, when I count to three, you run out the door and I'll be right behind you." He goes, "One, two, three," and opens the door. I start running and he starts running behind me.

Then, as soon as I got out, the sonofabitch slams the door behind me. I'm out there naked, yelling "Remember of Alamo" and I'm stuck there with nowhere to go. He hosed me good that time.

Bassett used to hang around with Bill and me a lot, and I'm telling you, we did some serious drinking and women chasing. Bill had saved up ten thousand dollars, working for Johnson & Johnson and we went through all of it in one year. We were totally wild.

In 1974, Alicia and I took a trip to Northern California to see her brother, and stopped at Los Alamitos, because I wanted to see this champion Quarter Horse named Kaweah Bar, who was my favorite horse. He was this gorgeous palomino, and his colors were blue and yellow with diamonds. I loved this horse so much, I eventually used that same color scheme and design for my own. On the way back, we stopped in Arcadia to see this aunt and uncle of hers. They lived right across the street from Santa Anita. Alicia wanted to go there, so we walked over to the track, and it was a rainy, miserable day. I had my camera with me, and there was Braulio Baeza and Laffit Pincay, and I was going, "Wow." It was my first real taste of Thoroughbred racing.

While I was at the University of Arizona, the Racetrack Industry Program came in there. I took it and found it easy, and Alicia thought it would be great for her and also signed up. She was ahead of me in units and graduated ahead of me. The summer before she graduated, she did an internship at Los Alamitos, working in different departments each week. She was one of the first ones to graduate from the program and intern at a racetrack, so they made a big deal out of it.

She told me I had to come out there. So I took these four ordinary horses and went to Los Alamitos to be with her. By the time I got out there, three weeks later, she already had another boyfriend. I was devastated. So now here I am at Los Alamitos with these four dogs, and what am I going to do now? I went back home and tried to get my life together.

The following year, after school was out, I returned to Los Alamitos with a friend, Jim Maple, and we had about five horses between us. My brother Bill also was there. I galloped the horses for Jim, who was a top trainer at Rillito Downs. Although they were his horses, I had a trainer's license at Los Alamitos, so they raced in my name. I wound up claiming a horse myself for two thousand dollars and was going to run him back. I couldn't win a race there, and wanted to win so badly before the meet ended. Four days before the end of the meet, I ran this horse, and a guy told me if he gave the horse some stuff the horse would win. I didn't know what it was and I barely knew the guy. At the time, I was sort of like a guinea pig, and he gave it to the horse. None of my horses ever got tested because they always ran so far back. So he gave this stuff to my horse, who still ended up losing, but they tested him on a spot check.

Now the meet's over and everybody has packed up and left. Maple's gone. Bill's gone. I'm waiting for my dad to come and get me when I get a call to go to the stable gate. They tell me I need to call the California Horse Racing Board. I call them and they tell me the horse I ran has tested positive for a pain killer. Well, it was like my guts had fallen out. I was so mad at myself. I kept thinking, "How stupid can I be?"

My dad shows up and I tell him the bad news. He was the listed owner of the horse, and he goes, "Bob, what's wrong with you?" But he felt bad for me; he knew I felt horrible. One thing about my dad, whenever I got in a bad spot, he'd never get on my case. He'd always say, "Don't worry, we'll deal with it." We drive up to Hollywood Park and my dad is trying to think of a story for me. We go before these investigators, and I do the usual deal: "I don't know what happened," and this and that. Afterward, they say, "We'll get back to you."

After going back home, I got a letter from the racing board saying I never showed up for my hearing. They had wanted me to go up to Sacramento because the meet was over. They told me if I came back in January, six months later, they'd give me a hearing. My dad typed out a story for me to tell — It was the last night of the meet, and a lot of horses were shipping out, and I noticed that there were a lot of suspicious characters hanging around the barn. With so many horses leaving at once, the security was kind of lax. This was my story. So I fly to Los Angeles, then on to Sacramento, with my typed up story. My sister Penny lived up there, and her husband, whom we called Happy, was going to law school at the time.

It was the first time I had ever been on a commercial plane. I get off in L.A., where I had an hour layover, and I don't know that they take the luggage from one plane to the other for you. I go downstairs to get my luggage and check it back in, and it never shows up. I start to panic. My whole goddamn story is in that bag. I finally go report it and give them all the information and tell them how important this bag is. Meanwhile, I can't leave L.A. without the bag. They ask me where I'm staying, and I tell them I'm supposed to be flying on to Sacramento. That's when they tell me it's already on the plane. Man, did I feel like a damn moron. What did I know? I grew up in Nogales.

So I fly up to Sacramento and I tell Happy about the fix I'm in, and I explain to him about the Absolute Insurer Rule, which states that trainers are responsible for any drug positives in their barn. And I show him my story. He takes everything upstairs and reads it for about an hour. At the time in L.A., the police were hunting for the Hillside Strangler and it was on the news every night. The next morning at breakfast, I ask Happy what he thinks. He says, "I read everything and I think I can get you off." I just lit up when he told me that. "Yeah, I think I found a loophole in this Insurer Rule," he says. "Just go in there and confess that you're the Hillside Strangler and they'll let you off on this."

Then he says, "I read your story, and, buddy, you don't have a prayer. Your only shot is to say that there was this Mexican guy who went by the name of 'El Groovo.' And instead of wearing those straps across his chest that held the bullets, he had syringes in there instead. Just tell them El Groovo got to your horse."

Penny got real mad at him for building up my hopes, and kidding around about it. The next day, she took me to the state capitol and they told me what I did was very serious, but I seemed like a nice kid. So they suspended me for a year, and made it retroactive. I had already done six months, and I really didn't care. I had been going to school and wasn't training anyway. I just wanted to get all this over with. I asked them if I could at least go to the races, as long as I kept off the backside, and they had no problem with that.

I continued to train horses on the ranch, and my dad still had a few horses in training. We had this barn at the track, and whenever we'd haul a horse to the track, my dad would hide me in the trailer when we came to the gate. After we got to the barn, I'd get out and get the horse ready, and stay in the barn. After we cooled the horse out, I'd get back in the trailer and leave. That's the way it went for the next six months.

While I had been at Los Alamitos with Jim Maple, I met Brad McKenzie. He was living in Cypress, California, and going to college while he was working as a groom for Barry Woodhouse. He was stabled right across from us. That was the beginning of a long friendship and some real wild times.

ARIZONA DAYS

"I've dragged Bobby out of some pretty dark places. I had to recover him from the bowels of iniquity. We'd drink whiskey together, and Bobby would start these fights with people, then disappear. He'd then come back and want a blow-by-blow description. Neither of us drink anymore. We stuffed sixty years of drinkin' into twenty, then quit. But back then, we were a couple of clowns who were totally out of control. We didn't take much serious then, and we still don't."   *— John Bassett*

When Brad McKenzie came to Arizona to go to the University of Arizona, my parents really got to like him and took him in as a member of the family. He actually went to work for John Bassett to make some extra money, but things didn't work out between them. One thing about John, he was a great guy, but he wasn't good to work for. He was pretty hard on you.

I had ridden for Bassett during the summers while I was going to school, and we won a few races together. But my main problem was that I couldn't switch sticks. I'd wind up dropping them. Bassett wasn't happy about it and would tell me, "Why don't you just pack two of 'em and forget it."

I remember one race up at the Arizona County Fair in Holbrook. I was riding one of his horses and we drew the one hole. They had shipped in a bunch of riders from Los Alamitos, and Robbie Bard, one of the top Quarter Horse riders, was one of them. He broke right next to me from the two hole, and I figured I'd just sit chilly and do what he did. He left there and started getting into his horse right-handed, so I got into my horse right-handed. He started hollerin' at his horse, so I hollered at my horse. He got his stick down and I got my stick down, and we were both rolling out there together on the lead. Just then, he switched sticks, so I switched sticks. And as I do, my stick goes flying halfway across the infield.

After the race, Bassett says to me, "Hey buddy, for us to stay friends, I got to fire you. You can't ride a hog in a phone booth."

He'd tell it like it was. One day, we were in his apartment and I was coming out of the shower. He looked at me and said, "Jesus Christmas, you look like something out of Dachau prison. Let me give you some advice. Give up riding and go get yourself a cheeseburger."

He was a character. One time, we rodeoed together in Tucson. In the team roping competition, I was on this horse who could stop on a dime. In team roping, the horse has to stop and go off to the left and pull the steer, so someone can come in and catch the steer. I told Bassett it was no problem, I could handle it. Well, the first one I ran, I stood up in the stirrups and flung my rope, and the damn horse disappeared from under me. I'm lying there on the ground and Bassett comes running out there hollering, "Safe!" I remember telling him, "Bassett, just get the hell away from me."

He always felt I was trying to embarrass him in front of other people, because I used to introduce him as my hick friend, John Bassett. One time, years later, he really got me back good. I was training Thoroughbreds by then, and we went to Keeneland to buy some yearlings. We attended a dinner party with Hal Earnhardt, who was one of my earliest clients and who introduced me to Mike Pegram. Among those in the party was Reba McEntire, the big country western singer. I was more into rock and didn't know that much about country music.

I wanted to impress her and show her I was familiar with her music, so I asked Bassett if she had a big hit out. He says, "Does she have a hit? Buddy, she's got a monster hit out right now." I ask him what the name is, so I can congratulate her on it, and he says, "It's called 'Big Balls in Cow Town.' It's Number Two right now and it's gonna be Number One." As we're leaving, I go up to her and say, "I want to congratulate you on that great song, 'Big Balls in Cow Town.'" She looks at me and says, "Pardon me?" Man, did I feel like an idiot. I knew he had gotten me, and I just yelled to him, "Bassett, you sonofabitch." She actually thought it was pretty funny.

After graduating college, I was still on suspension, so I did some substitute teaching in Nogales — from first grade to high school. I worked for thirty bucks a day, five days a week. We had a house up in Tucson, and I'd go up there on weekends and blow my whole check. They stuck me teaching full time when one of the teachers flipped out and showed up one day with some rifles in his car. He was planning on shooting everybody. I filled in for two weeks until they found somebody, but they couldn't find anyone. The principal was going out with my aunt, and he said he was desperate and need-ed me for the rest of the semester. I told him I wasn't a teacher, and he just said, "You can do it." I taught history in junior high, and I had to sit up and read that damn book every night.

They stuck me with the real bad class, and there were some bad-ass troublemakers in there. The first thing they told me was that I had to pass every kid, because they were getting too old to be in junior high. My first day, I turned around to write something on the black-board, and I got bombarded by spitballs. I said to myself, "I think I've got a situation here." What I did was pick out the toughest kid in the class. I told him, "You're going to be my sergeant-at-arms. If anybody gets out of hand, you go over and whack them in the head." But I told him if he was going to be my disciplinarian, he had to do the work. He had been a bad student, but he got so into it he started reading. Anytime someone would get out of hand, I'd say, "Go get him," and he'd go over there and slap the kid over the head. I had everything under control, and he became my buddy. He loved me. The class started going so smoothly, and everyone began studying.

After junior high, I taught high school. I had a deal with the kids. I told them, "I don't care what you do in here, but if that door opens, I want everyone to shut down what you're doing and look down at your book and act like you're doing your work. That's all I ask." One time, it was loud as hell in there, and all of a sudden, the door starts to open, and everyone drops everything and buries their head in their book. The principal looks in and goes, "Oh, okay." Later he tells me, "Boy, you have them trained pretty good." Horses or people, I was always training one way or another. They even voted me Teacher of the Month one time, and I was only a substitute, and basically a kid myself.

The following summer, I put a small string of our horses together and went to Prescott Downs, and I was going to start training again. Prescott, Arizona, is a fun town, and my dad put me up in a little cabin there. One of the horses we had was named Pete Hoist, who eventually made me quit training and almost ruined me as a Quarter Horse trainer. Pete Hoist kept running the fastest qualifying times in the trials, but always found a way to lose in the finals.

My father had never won a stakes race with one of his horses. I ran Pete Hoist in a trial for the Prescott Futurity and he had the fastest qualifying time. I ran him back in the finals and he finished second. He broke the track record in the Holbrook Futurity trial and you couldn't find him in the finals. Then I ran him in the trials for the Globe Futurity and he again had the fastest qualifying time. But in the finals, he broke badly and finished eighth. What made it even worse was that Bassett kept beating me in the finals with his horse Reb Space Captain. I said, "That's it, I'm done. I can't take this anymore." I felt I couldn't win the big one, so I got the hell out.

There was another incident at Prescott I'll never forget. I saw my friend Mitch DeGroot's wife killed in a spill and it was just horrible. She was breezing a horse, and he ducked in and hit the rail. She fell off and hit one of the goose necks (the curved portion of the bars that support the rail) and was killed instantly. I can still visualize her laying there with the rail wrapped around her. Man, it was terrible.

I returned to Nogales and turned the horses out. I substitute taught a little bit, then got a job working at Walco, a veterinary supply company in Tucson. I worked from eight in the morning until five and was making eight hundred a month. I was kickin' ass. I'd hang around and go to the races on the weekends. My dad was running a couple of horses here and there, and I was still involved a little, helping him out once in a while. But I didn't want to have anything to do with it.

While I was in Tucson working at Walco, I hung around with Brad and Bill, and we'd spend a lot of time at the Vineyard, a restaurant that P. A. and Dee Dee ran. That's where I met my wife Sherry, who was a cocktail waitress there. She was without a doubt the worst waitress I'd even seen. We'd always have lunches there for free, and we'd be eating and drinking and having a good time. Sherry would come over and say, "You guys don't want *another* drink, do you?"

We used to terrorize poor P. A. They had a live lobster tank there, and Brad and I used to cut the rubber bands holding the claws, then watch the waiters reach in and try to get those sonofaguns. Sometimes, we would float Big Macs in the tank. When someone would order a lobster and the waiter would take them back to put them in the boiling water, we would stand behind the kitchen door and make these sounds like a lobster screaming.

We had nothing to do. We'd just hang around playing Pac Man every day. The Vineyard was the meeting place where we'd all get together. I had met Sherry the year before and asked her out, but she said she couldn't go. I was dating a friend of her roommate's at the time, and I was one of those guys who would ask a girl out about four hours before the date. After I broke up with this other girl, Sherry and I started dating. We wound up going out for four years before getting married in 1984.

During the summer, around the end of the Rillito meet, I was offered a job by Pete Sammons, who owned horses and had his own farm in Prescott. I told him I would work for him under one condition: I didn't want to train horses. I just wanted to run his farm. He agreed, so I went to Prescott and was in charge of five broodmares and five yearlings and one stud named Mito. Sherry had graduated from the University of Arizona and moved to Phoenix. Eventually, she would come to Prescott for the weekends and we'd go to the races.

One day, Pete asked me if I could find him a horse at Los Alamitos to run in the Prescott Futurity. I bought him a horse named Bishop Cat, who was a high-priced claimer and low-level allowance horse, and we trained him at the farm. I bought him from a guy named Judd Morse, who was a great person and real party guy. We got him ready for the Futurity and had Bobby Adair, one of the great Quarter Horse riders, come to ride him.

A week before the Futurity, Pete was away and wasn't expected back until the following day. I was supposed to be breaking these five yearlings. There was one filly who was really tough, so we hired this guy to work with her and take the buck out of her. Brad and Bill came in and we decided to go play golf. When we got back, I saw Pete's motor home parked in front of the house. He had gotten back a day early. The vet's truck was also there, and I thought, "Uh oh."

The filly had flipped and tried to jump out of her stall. She cut herself pretty badly and the vet was there to stitch her back up. I told Brad and Bill to leave everything to me. I told them to just walk calmly up to the house and not say anything. I went over to Pete, and he asked me, "Where the hell have you been?" I said we had just gone out for some lunch. Just then, we hear all this noise on the gravel road. We look up and there are Brad and Bill walking to the house still wearing their golf shoes. Pete got really hot that I took the day off to play golf, but he calmed down once he realized the filly was going to be alright.

Judd Morse had come out to see the race, and the night before, we all decided to take him and Bobby Adair out for a good time. It was me, Bill, Brad, and Bassett. Bill had known this girl who was Miss Rodeo Arizona, and we borrowed her pick-up truck and took them to this club in Prescott. Judd and Bobby were not afraid to have a drink or two with you. In fact, Judd used to drink martinis and call them silver bullets. So, we drank and danced and partied all night and closed the place down. Judd and Bobby were staying at a Holiday Inn, and with the amount of drinking they did, we took them back to the hotel to make sure they got there okay.

It was about three in the morning when we got back. Judd and Bobby were getting kind of loud, and we were trying to get them to their hotel room without causing too much attention. The parking lot was on an incline, and Bill had forgotten to set the parking brake in the pick-up. Just as we got them out of the truck, we looked back to see the truck rolling down this hill and heading toward a tin tool shed where the hotel stored their wheelbarrows and other equipment. The truck plowed into the shed, and there were all these rakes and pitchforks flying all over the place. I think we woke everyone in the whole damn hotel up. We got the hell out of there as fast as we could. The next day, we ran Bishop Cat in the Futurity and he was beaten a neck.

I then took Bishop Cat to Globe, Arizona, for the Futurity and he qualified, then ran second in the Futurity. During that time, there were a couple of trainers who had horses test positive. One of them, a friend of mine named Ray Yeigh, asked me, "If I get suspended, do you want to take over my horses while I'm away?" He was a real character, but he had a lot of good horses, so I started thinking seriously about it. It was starting to get cold in Prescott, and I really didn't want to stay on the farm any longer. I went to the hearing to see what they gave the two of them. The first guy, Owen McDaniel, who was one of the leading Quarter Horse trainers in the state, got a year's suspension, and he came out and didn't talk to anybody. He just got in his car and drove away. Then Ray Yeigh came out and I asked him, "So, what did they give you?" He looked at me and said, "Well, Bob, they told me I got three days to get out of Dodge."

I quit working for Pete and went to Tucson and set up the stable at Rillito Downs. That same day, I picked up some horses from Owen McDaniel's clients. They saw what I had done turning Bishop Cat from a claimer to a stakes horse and decided to give me some horses. Before I accepted the job, I had done some thinking. The only reason I took Ray Yeigh's horses and went to training again was that I always felt I was missing something. I had never won a big race — a Futurity or any other kind of stakes. There was this void in my life, and I decided to train these horses just until I won a major race, then I'd quit and do something else. I still had that feeling gnawing at me that I couldn't win the big one.

I realized afterward that the reason I couldn't win the big one was because I was training for my dad, who really didn't have good stock. As soon as I got away from him and picked up all those Ray Yeigh horses, I started kickin' ass. I won three races, including a stakes, the very first day. By the end of the first year, I was the leading trainer at Rillito. I had a filly I had broken for Pete Sammons named Kellys Coffer, and she wound up winning everything in Arizona. She was my first big horse, and won about a dozen races as a two-year-old.

I was in the same barn as Vern Goodman, who had a private barn and let me stable my horses there. His father Rulon was one of the top horsemen in the country, and he ran Rillito, leasing it from the county. Rulon was the one who kept the track going. He's the guy Brad McKenzie was working for when I met him. Sherry had a little savings account and I borrowed six-hundred dollars from her to get started and paid her back thirty days later. She's never let me forget that. She always tells me, "Remember, buddy, I'm the one who lent you money to get started."

Vern was a good friend whom I had known for years and we always had a good time together. I had Kellys Coffer and Vern had Love N Money, who I eventually took over the following year when Vern decided to give up training. They ran against each other in this one big two-year-old race. There's this superstition around the racetrack that you never pee in a horse's stall the day he's running. Sometimes, if there isn't a bathroom around and you have to go, it's easier to go in the horse's stall. But if you do it the day the horse is in, it's bad luck and he won't win. Vern had this girl who was working for him, and I said, "You know what, I'm going to find out if this superstition really works." So, the day of the race, when Vern left, I went in Love N Money's stall and peed in there.

Well, Love N Money goes out and beats Kellys Coffer a nose, and after the race, I go over to Vern and say, "I guess that superstition about peeing in a horse's stall is all wrong." He asks me what I mean, and I tell him, "I peed in Love N Money's stall this morning." He said, "That's okay. When I got back, I found out what you did, so I went and peed in Kellys Coffer's stall." He neutralized my ass. But that's how close we were. You wouldn't do that unless you were good friends.

The following year, Vern got tired of training and moved to Utah and opened a Western tack shop. Before he left, he told me he talked to his dad and they agreed I could take over his horses. Rulon was a good old man, but he was tough. He came from the old school. He started in the grocery business where every dime was important. Wayne Lukas actually trained for him for a while.

Wayne told me one time that Rulon had asked him if he wanted-ed to go on a roundup. He thought it would be great playing cowboy, eating at the chuck wagon, and having a nice trailer to sleep in. After all, the guy was a multimillionaire with a chain of grocery stores. So, Wayne went on this roundup, and after one day of sleeping in a sleeping bag and eating peanut butter and jelly sandwiches, he got the hell out of there. That's just the way Rulon was. When you won, he never said thank you or congratulated you. He just felt you were privileged to work for him. He was always good to me, but after a year, he quit the racetrack. He just lost all interest after Vern left.

By now, I had built up my stable to thirty horses. I went to Prescott, and Sherry and I moved in together. I started winning everything. I had Kellys Coffer and a real good horse named Twin Profit for Barry Woodhouse. He was a pretty good three-year-old in California, and Barry wanted him to become a stakes winner, so he sent him to me to try to win the Prescott Derby, which he did. I was in a tight race

I gave my school picture (above) to a girl I liked in elementary school. Clockwise, from top left, Norie, Penny, me, Dee Dee, and P. A. My first communion (below).

Me and P. A. on horseback (left); at the county fair with Gamble (on a 4-H steer), Bill behind him, and me holding the lead; winning with Baffert's Heller in 1964 (bottom); front row: P. A., me, and cousin John Baffert; back row: Blain Lewis, Iree Lewis, uncle Phil Baffert, and my father. I was already exercising our racehorses at age eleven. Notice my bowed legs.

My first win as a jockey (above) on
Sizzling Snark; weighing in, 1971;
I broke all the horses at our ranch,
including the one I'm on below.

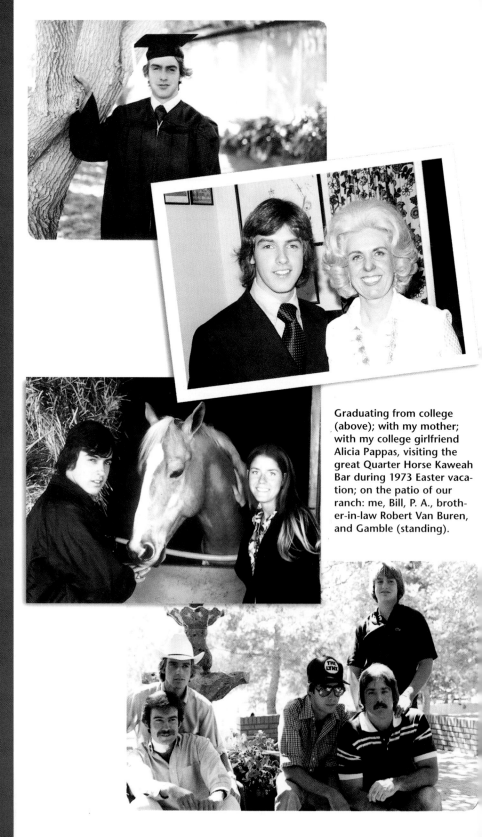

Graduating from college (above); with my mother; with my college girlfriend Alicia Pappas, visiting the great Quarter Horse Kaweah Bar during 1973 Easter vacation; on the patio of our ranch: me, Bill, P. A., brother-in-law Robert Van Buren, and Gamble (standing).

Winning my first Thoroughbred stakes as a trainer (above), in 1982 at Rillito Downs; my first win at Los Alamitos, (middle) in 1983 with Five OClock Rush; me breezing Pete Hoist at Rillito.

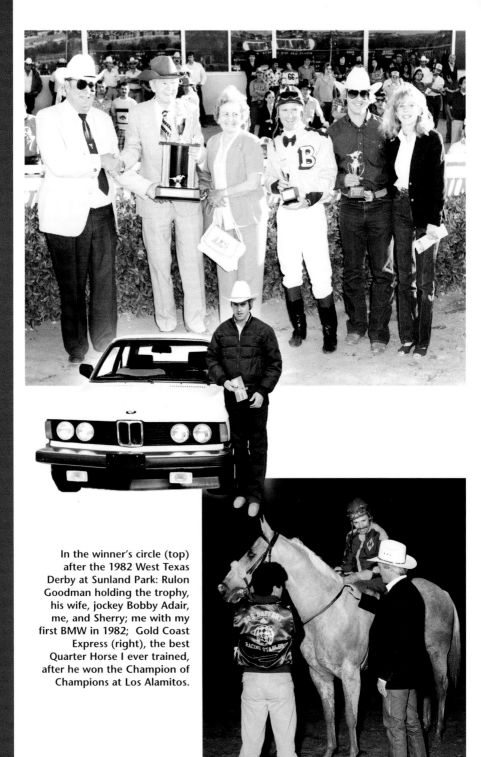

In the winner's circle (top) after the 1982 West Texas Derby at Sunland Park: Rulon Goodman holding the trophy, his wife, jockey Bobby Adair, me, and Sherry; me with my first BMW in 1982; Gold Coast Express (right), the best Quarter Horse I ever trained, after he won the Champion of Champions at Los Alamitos.

Me, Sherry, and P. A. at our wedding in December of 1984; Brad McKenzie, P. A., me, and dad on my wedding day (top right); the baptism of our first child, Taylor; Our four children, from left: Canyon, Savannah, Taylor, and Forest; (below) me and Sherry at the 1998 Kentucky Derby.

In the winner's circle at Gulfstream Park (above) in 1992, after Thirty Slews (middle) wins the Sprint; me and my "main man," Mike Pegram, who got me into Thoroughbreds.

Me and the Monsignor (top) cheering for Cavonnier, who loses by a nose to Grindstone in the 1996 Kentucky Derby. We go on to the Preakness, where Cavonnier is about to work (left); I communicate with my exercise rider with a two-way radio (above).

Silver Charm, winning the Del Mar Futurity (left); taking the Charm to the track before the '97 Derby (below), which he won by a nose over Captain Bodgit (bottom); the next morning, I meet the press (below left).

A quiet moment at Pimlico (left); Beverly Lewis is cracking up when I goof off after we win the Preakness; I really felt the love from the Belmont crowd (below); walking from the Belmont tunnel to the paddock (bottom) before the Belmont Stakes; at the Belmont draw with my daughter Savannah (left).

MR. BAFFERT: DO YOU BELIEVE IN DESTINY?

VISA

In the 1998 Dubai World Cup, the Charm holds off Swain (above); Sheikh Mo and Bob Lewis crowning me after the race; decked out in Arab garb after returning to the U.S.

Making "the walk" on Derby Day 1998 (top); Mike's grandson, Gator, giving a rose to Kent Desormeaux; in the winner's circle (left); and below, where we probably had the largest crowd in history.

Giving instructions to Kent Desormeaux (left) before the '98 Preakness; Victory Gallop winning the Belmont Stakes by a nod (below), spoiling our second Triple Crown bid. Sherry, Savannah, and I reacting to the Belmont finish.

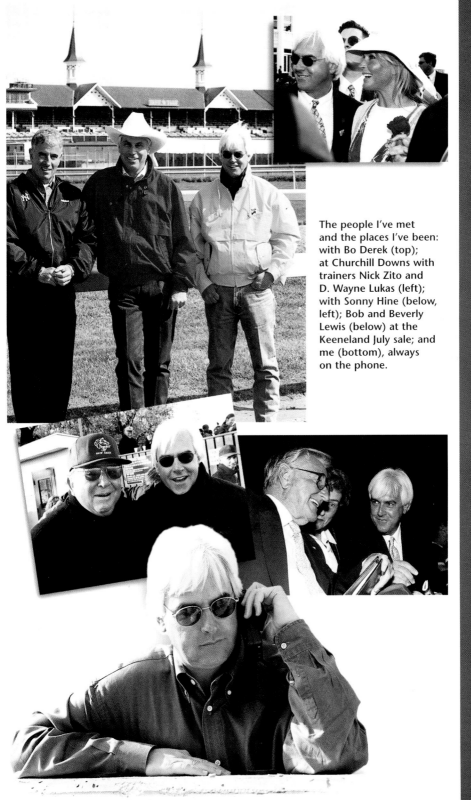

The people I've met and the places I've been: with Bo Derek (top); at Churchill Downs with trainers Nick Zito and D. Wayne Lukas (left); with Sonny Hine (below, left); Bob and Beverly Lewis (below) at the Keeneland July sale; and me (bottom), always on the phone.

Meeting Ken Griffey Jr. (above); in my
Austin Powers outfit (above right)
before the '99 Hollywood Gold Cup;
with Aaron and Marie Jones (right)
and Jerry Bailey after Forestry's win in
the Dwyer; in the trainers' stand with
Sheikh Mo (below right) during Derby
week; winning an Eclipse Award as
leading trainer (below);
and Silverbulletday, the best filly
I ever trained.

for the training title, so I wanted to run Twin Profit one more time at Prescott. I talked to Barry and told him I'd like to keep him there for one more race and he agreed. The horse didn't break well, and coming out of the gate, he got hit in the eye with a rock.

An infection set in, and he wound up losing the eye. As it turned out, the horse didn't even win and I didn't even need him to win the title. I opened up a big lead on this other guy and won it easily. He was a neat horse and he was doing good at the time, and it was just a freak deal.

Another awful experience happened with a horse I had named Wheelin Ernie, who was a tough, old $2,500 claimer. The fellow who owned him was a real nice guy, and he had brought in these partners to get them interested in racing. I had two horses entered in the Prescott Futurity, and the owner wanted to run Ernie in a small stakes on the card. I didn't want to do it, because Ernie was an old gelding who would have had to run hard in a race like that. Well, I finally gave in and Ernie ran his guts out and finished third.

He gets back to the barn and drops dead of a heart attack. Now, I've got these two horses to saddle in the Futurity, and when I get to the grandstand, the owner is there with all the partners and their families and all these little kids, and they want to go back to the barn and see Ernie. I don't know how to break the news to them, so I just tell them it wasn't a good time. All the kids then start yelling, "We want to see Ernie. We want to see Ernie." By now, the owner is getting upset and insists on seeing Ernie. Meanwhile, it's almost time to saddle for the big race and I try again to convince him not to go, but the guy is starting to get real mad, telling me it's his horse and he wants to see him. Finally, I have to go saddle the horses and I can't take it any longer, so I just snap back at the guy, 'Hey, buddy, Ernie's dead, okay?' All the kids started crying, and I felt terrible. That was one awful scene.

The year before, in 1982, I had been looking to drum up some more business, so I drove with Brad to the All American yearling sale in Ruidoso, New Mexico. Brad's mom had just gotten this big, white Cadillac, and he drove from Los Alamitos, where he was working as assistant publicity director, to Prescott to pick me up. We took turns driving, and when it was my turn, I was haulin' ass, going around 90 miles an hour. The car had one of those digital odometers that started blinking if it went over eighty-five. When Brad drove, I told him I was going to take a nap, and when I woke up, I wanted to see that odometer blinking.

While I'm sleeping, Brad gets stopped for speeding and winds up getting a ticket. About five minutes later, I wake up and see that he's going sixty and start chewing him out. He told me he had just gotten a ticket, but all I was interested in was getting to the sale, so I said to him, "Well, you already got your ticket, chances are you won't get another one."

We finally got to the sale, and neither of us had much money. I saw this well-bred filly in the ring named Apollina who I liked, and she was going real cheap. I wound up buying her for eleven-thousand dollars using the money I had saved to buy Sherry an engagement ring. It was blood money. Driving back, I was trying to figure out how I was going to break the news to Sherry. I was thinking of changing the filly's name to Sherry's Honeymoon, but you couldn't change the name once it had been registered. The year before, I had bought her a Rolex, and I was hoping that would hold her for a while. As it turned out, she was okay with it. When I told her what I had done, all she said was "I just hope it's a good one."

The first time I ran Apollina was the following May in the Sonoita Futurity trials. She had been working really well, but I think I might have trained her a little too light. She broke out of the gate and went about fifty yards and started bucking. She bucked all the way down the racetrack and ran dead last. I was embarrassed as hell. Thank God I owned her and didn't have to explain it to anybody. I took her to Prescott, and although she still wanted to buck, she qualified for the Prescott Futurity. I ran her in the Futurity and she finished second. That was two races after Wheelin Ernie died. I didn't have much equipment at the time, so I had to pull the ring bit from Wheelin Ernie's mouth and put it in Apollina's mouth. She earned about ten thousand dollars for finishing second, and then I sold her to her original owner for thirty thousand. That was my escape to Los Al. My days in Arizona were over.

CHAMPION OF CHAMPIONS

"When Bob made the move from Arizona to Los Alamitos, we got married and I started having children. What I didn't like about it was Bob's schedule. He never went to the barn quite as early as everyone else, but once he got there, he'd hang around, then go out to lunch. He'd come home and take a nap and have dinner, then it would be time to go back to the track for the races, and he'd be gone until late at night. After our son Taylor was born, I remember being super lonely on the weekends watching all the families together with their kids, and it was just me and Taylor." — *Sherry Baffert*

In the winter of 1983, I decided to finally make the big move to Los Alamitos. Each summer at Prescott, I'd say, "What the hell am I doing here?" But I couldn't go to Los Al, because the racing secretary there, Curley Smith, was too tough, especially with someone new. You just couldn't get stalls there. He ruled the roost and controlled everybody like the Gestapo. But that year, he was replaced by Pete Drypolcher, who was a good guy and more understanding of the horsemen.

Brad had told Pete he had this buddy who was the dominant trainer in Arizona and was looking to come to Los Al for the winter. But he needed enough stalls to make it worthwhile. Pete assured Brad that if I brought good horses, he'd give me the stalls. Most of my brothers and sisters had already moved to California, so I was pretty thrilled about it.

I had about thirty horses in training, and I picked my ten best and shipped them to Los Al for the opening of the meet. After three weeks, I couldn't win a race, and I was really getting discouraged. Everything I sent out was running second, third, or fourth. Here I was, the king dog back in Arizona, and I couldn't do a damn thing here. Finally, I made a decision that could have changed the entire course of my life. It was a Friday night, and I entered my five best horses. I told Brad, "If I don't win a race tonight, I'm going home." I was dead serious. I ran the first four horses and could only manage a couple of seconds.

I was down to my last horse, a good, honest allowance filly named Five OClock Rush. After I saddled her, Brad came down from the press box, and P. A. was there as well. I told them, "This is it. If she doesn't win, I'm packing my shit and I'm leaving. This is too tough for me. I can't handle it."

Five OClock Rush had drawn the one-hole and I almost scratched her, but I left her in. She hits the wire in a three-horse photo, and we've got to sweat it out. Finally, they put her number up. So it was Five OClock Rush's nose that kept me at Los Alamitos instead of retreating to Arizona.

When the winter meet ended, I did go back to Arizona instead of taking the horses up to Bay Meadows, but it was only to regroup. I returned to Los Al in the summer, and I told my clients we had to start claiming some horses. I brought about fifteen head with me, and the rest I claimed. I have to admit, I made some really lucky claims. I had pretty good success that summer and I stayed for good. Bassett sent me some talented horses who were way too good to run at Prescott, including a very talented horse named Neats Wonder, and that really helped me get going.

Bassett was training for Hal Earnhardt, and that's how I met

Hal. The first horse I trained for him was named Miss Bud Light. How about that? Who'd ever think I'd go from Miss Bud Light to Bob Lewis, who was the largest Budweiser distributor in California?

Everything was going great, but the best was yet to come. I was about to experience a feeling I thought I would never have again in my life. Sherry and I were married, and we had bought a home in Huntington Beach. There was this owner named Bill Mitchell who had a really good two-year-old named Gold Coast Express, a colt I had beaten one day. Bill was a big, old friendly kind of guy who liked to talk to everybody, and we were just hanging around bullshitting after that race. I really thought nothing of it.

About six months later, I got a message at the stable gate to call Bill Mitchell. Back in Arizona, I had trained for this guy from San Diego named Mitchell, who had sent me some buckskin horses to train, and they were a bunch of dogs. I noticed the area code on the message was 619, which is San Diego, so I thought it had to be the same Mitchell. I decided not to call him back. The next day, there were more messages from Bill Mitchell, and I still didn't call. It was ironic, but the day before, I was with my jockey, Kip Didericksen, and we just happened to be talking about Gold Coast Express. He was a helluva horse who had won the Blue Ribbon Futurity the year before, but he never had any luck in the finals. You could spot him easily, because he was a palomino, and everyone knew him as the yellow horse. He'd always qualify the fastest in the trials, but something would always happen in the finals to cost him the race.

The guy who trained him was named Lee Glad. He had just worked the horse two days in a row because he didn't like the way the jockey had worked him the first day. He felt he had gone too slow. I was standing there with Kip, and I told him, "Goddamn, can you imagine having a horse like this? Man, would I love to have this horse." He had come back as a three-year-old, and Glad ran him against older horses and he beat them. You just don't run three-year-olds against older horses early in the year, never mind beat them.

So the next day I get a call and it's Bill Mitchell, and he wants to know how come I haven't returned his calls. I'm thinking it's this other guy in San Diego, and I tell him, "Oh yeah, I just got your message. I was just about to call you." He says to me, "You got room for some more horses?" And I go, "Well, yeah, what do you got?" He's thinking, "What a cocky sonofabitch."

He starts rattling off the names of his horses, and he goes, "And of course, there's the yellow horse." I'm going, "Yellow horse?" Then I realize that I recognize the names he's rattling off. In fact, I almost claimed one of them from him. Thank God, I didn't. When he mentions the yellow horse, I say to him "Wait a minute, you mean Gold Coast Express?" And he says yes. I go, "Oh, you're that Bill Mitchell!" I ask him why he wants to switch trainers, being the horse just beat older horses in a stakes race.

He told me he liked Lee Glad, and that Lee's father had trained for him, but he and his wife felt the horse should have won more big races the year before, and maybe Gold Coast Express was too much horse for him. He said he hated to do it, but the horse looked like he was coming back great and he wanted to send him to someone new. He said if he didn't give him to me, he had someone else he was going to give him to. I said I'd be happy to take him, and he told me not to say anything to Lee, because he wanted to tell him himself.

When I hung up the phone, I told Sherry, "I don't believe it. This guy just gave me Gold Coast Express." I felt like I had just hit the lottery. I went to the barn that afternoon and talked to my veterinarian, Nancy Goodman, who had just started doing work for Glad. I told her, "Nancy, don't say anything, but they're giving me

Gold Coast Express, and I know you know the horse. Is there improvement there?" And she said, "Oh yeah, there's a lot of improvement." She told me Glad already knew he was losing the horses, but he didn't know who was getting them.

The next morning, the word was out. Mitchell had sent his manager out there to move the horses. When I got to the barn, somebody told me, "Hey, Lee Glad is looking for you." Glad was from Oklahoma, and he was one big dude. I knew this was a touchy deal, but I always got along with the guy. There was so much jealousy, people wanted to make it sound like I stole the horse away from him. But he knew I hadn't. If he did think that, he probably would have slapped me around. When the manager showed up, he told me to go get the horses, and I said, "Shit, I ain't going there. You go get them."

When I got the horse, he was in good shape. I ran him at Hollywood Park and left his rider Danny Cardoza on him. I was really nervous running him for the first time, but this horse was so awesome. There have been only two horses who really made an impact on my life: Silver Charm and Gold Coast Express. They were two totally different types, but both would barely win. Gold Coast Express would bust out of there and take the lead, then just eyeball the others down. He truly was a great horse.

I won five in a row with him. Then I ran him in the Hollywood Park Championship and he finished second to Cash Rate, who was the champion older horse. That qualified him to run in the Champion of Champions at Los Alamitos in December. It was a $200,000 purse and was considered the Breeders' Cup Classic of Quarter Horse racing. It was the most prestigious race in the country for three-year-olds and up, and you had to beat every top horse.

After the Hollywood race, I didn't run him for two months. I wanted him to come into the race fresh. Even the owner started getting a little apprehensive when he found out I was going to train him up to the race. I told him, "This is what I want to do. We won all these races and were beaten one time by Cash Rate. If we freshen him up and get him right, I think we can win it and get World Champion," which is the equivalent of Horse of the Year. I assured him I'd get him ready.

So I just sat on him. In the last couple of weeks the owner started asking people if they thought we were doing the right thing. Everyone was telling him, "I don't know. That's a helluva long layoff." He wound up going off as third choice, because a lot of people probably thought there was something wrong with him.

But when those gates opened, he just scalded away from there. It was a wet track and everything went perfect for us that night. He opened up about two lengths on 'ol Cash Rate. At the end, Cash Rate was running him down, but he ran out of ground and we beat him a nose. When he hit the wire, I thought, "It will not get any better than this. This is it. I have hit the pinnacle of my career." I ran down there and I was going crazy. I mean it was huge. This was a race even Lukas never won.

That night, we went to this bar across the street from the track called Alejandro's. We were dancing all night and getting up to the microphone and fooling around. That was around the time the movie *Ghostbusters* was out, so my brothers got up to the mike and they started shouting, "We came. We saw. We kicked their ass."

Every time Gold Coast Express won, I'd come out to the parking lot and there would be this long key scratch down the side of my car. By the time we left the bar that night, I had done some serious drinking. I had just bought a brand new Ford Bronco, and when we came out, I took one look at it and said, "Am I that drunk or does my car look like it's leaning off to the side?" When we got up to it, I saw that the covering on the spare tire in the back was cut in half, and the tires on the right side were completely flat, with all these slash marks on them. At first I was pissed, but if that was the price I had to pay to win the Champion of Champions, it was worth it.

Winning the Champion of Champions really helped my business. In fact, I wound up winning it again a couple of years later with a horse named Shawnes Favorite, whom I had bought privately for $150,000 after he ran second to me in the Los Alamitos Derby.

I had adapted really nicely to the California scene. We had a house by the beach, and I'd play my guitar. But I still always wore my cowboy hat. In April of 1986, our first child, Taylor, was born. Then two years later, in June of 1988, we had Canyon. Forest was born in December of 1990, and our daughter Savannah came in September of 1993.

I was doing great. I won every Futurity and Derby at Los Alamitos and had reached the pinnacle of my profession. There was no way I could imagine that my success was only beginning and that I was about to embark on a journey that would take me to places I never even dreamed of. And it all came about by meeting one person: Mike Pegram.

MAIN MAN

"The first time I went to a sale with Bobby was in Ruidoso, New Mexico, and he really wanted this horse badly. I was going in as a partner with Hal Earnhardt and his father Tex, whom I had gotten to know really well. When Hal backed out, Bobby was really upset, and he was walking around there, kickin' and bitchin'. I told him, 'Hey bud, I don't know you from a load of coal, but I got my own damn money. If you want to buy something, you buy it. You don't have to worry about that crap with me.' I can tell right off the bat if I like somebody, and there was no bullshit about Bobby. He wound up buying me some horse that night for $20,000, but the horse had been standing in deep shavings, and Bobby couldn't see that there was something wrong with his feet. After the sale, he told me he'd like to go partners with me on the horse. Unbeknownst to me at the time, the reason he wanted to go partners was because he knew he had made a bad buy and had damaged goods on his hands. It became obvious to me at that point, this was a guy who was going to take care of people, and it really showed me he was accountable." — Mike Pegram

Hal Earnhardt and I were at the 1985 September yearling sale at Ruidoso, and there was this Dash For Cash colt we were interested in. Dash For Cash was the hottest Quarter Horse sire in the country. I was never one to pay much money for a horse, but I felt this colt was going to bring some money — at least forty or fifty grand. Hal told me his father Tex was really good friends with this great guy

107

named Mike Pegram, who owned all these McDonald's franchises. At the time, Mike was going out with Hal's sister Debbie, off and on.

So Hal gets on his phone and calls Mike and asks him if he'd like to get involved in part of this Dash For Cash colt. Mike had some Thoroughbreds with his dad, and he had others with a partner named Bob Roth. After Mike got divorced in 1982, he had given up the horses. But when he began hanging around with Hal and Tex, he became exposed to Quarter Horses and started going with them to the bush tracks in Arizona.

Hal told Mike this horse was going to bring some pretty good money, and Mike was thinking he meant around $200,000. He agreed to go in for half, and we got the horse for $60,000. The colt's name was Entourage, and we broke him and got him ready for a race at Bay Meadows. Then I sent him down to Los Alamitos for this little stakes, and that's where I first met Mike.

We tried to figure out how we were going to find each other, and I told him I'd be wearing a white Resistol cowboy hat and my hair was turning white. He told me he'd have his girlfriend with him, and that she was tall, blonde, and beautiful. So Mike got to the track and everybody was wearing a white Resistol cowboy hat. He looked all over, but had no way of finding me. As it turned out, I found him. Everyone might have been wearing the same cowboy hat, but not everyone had a girl who looked like that.

Entourage wound up dead-heating for the win. I ran the horse a few more times, and he won the Kindergarten consolation, but he didn't turn out to be the great horse I thought he would. We came out all right on him and got our money back, but he certainly was no monster or anything like that.

That summer, Mike, Hal, and I went to the Ruidoso sale. I hadn't been around Mike that much and didn't really know him very well. All night long, I wanted to buy this one colt, and we thought he'd bring about twenty-five or thirty grand. Hal was doing all the bidding. He's a great guy, but he's very conservative. He's got testicles the size of acorns. But I don't blame him, because mine are the same size. When the bidding got up to $30,000, I could see who we were going against and I knew he was tough. He had a good eye for a horse. I said to Hal, "Whatever you do, don't weaken. Don't give this guy any indication you're weakening."

We were bidding one thousand and two thousand at a time, but when the bidding got up to forty thousand, Hal started upping it five hundred dollars a pop. I told him, "Don't do that shit," and Mike said, "Come on, hit him again. Go up there." Hal turned to Mike and said, "It's easy for you to say, you're only in for a third." Well, Mike thought he was in for half, and when he found out it was only for a third, along with Hal and Tex, he got a little upset. If I had known Mike a little better at the time, I would have told him to just keep on going. Needless to say, we didn't get the horse. His name was Runaway Winner, and he went on to earn about $400,000.

I bitched all night about not getting the horse, and finally, Mike told me if I saw something I liked, he had his own money and I should go ahead and buy it. We missed the good horse, so I wound up buying this other horse for Mike who was some cheapy named Masked Boy. We just saw him in the back of the ring, and they had really deep shavings in there. Afterward, I noticed the horse was really crooked in the back from the ankle down. I felt really bad about it and offered to go partners with Mike, but he said, "Don't worry about it."

After the sale, Mike wanted to get out of Ruidoso real bad. He just wanted out of there. He said, "I've had enough of this place," and he rented a car to drive to El Paso. Mike's the kind of guy, when he wants out of a situation, he wants out. I told him, "Hell, I want out of here, too." I was still upset we didn't get that horse. There were horses selling there for $200,000 and $300,000, but he was the one. He was the sleeper of the sale.

So I hopped in the car and rode with Mike to El Paso, where we would catch a plane home. It was about an hour and a half drive, and as it turned out, we knew a lot of the same people, and we really hit if off. When we got to the airport, we couldn't get any flights to L.A., and Mike said he had no intention of spending the night in El Paso. He told me, "I might end up in Dallas, or I might end up in Chicago. I might have to go the wrong way to get where I want to go, but I sure as hell ain't staying here." I said, "I'm with you."

Mike then asked me if I wanted to go to Las Vegas, and I told him I'd never been there before. He said, "Come on, we'll fly to Vegas and spend the night there." I called Sherry and told her what was going on. I said I was with a new client and that he was going to be really big. She said, "Sure, Bob, sure." She wasn't buying it. She never believed shit I told her anyway.

So we got on the flight and went to Vegas. We checked into the hotel, and Mike went down to the casino and started shooting craps. I watched him drop five grand in the first five minutes and I couldn't take it, so I just walked off. He told me to come back in twenty minutes. I came back and watched him lose another two throws. When he realized twenty minutes were up, he stopped. The next thing I knew, they were writing him a voucher for fifty grand. I couldn't believe it — fifty grand! He said, "Well, that gets me even from the last time I was here."

They put us in this suite, and I had never seen anything like it. It had this huge living room and a baby grand piano and a Jacuzzi. Mike had some friends he knew there, and they showed up with these girls. One of them rode horses and wanted to be a rodeo queen. The next thing I know, I'm in the Jacuzzi with everyone, wearing my cowboy hat and drinking Budweiser. Mike had been doing some business on the phone, and he walked in with his beer in his hand, looked at me in the Jacuzzi, and said, "I think this is going to turn out to be a good relationship. The two of us are going to go places together."

I kept training some Quarter Horses for him through 1986, but it was just nickel and dime stuff. The following year, Mike's father died and that was pretty rough on him. His father had twenty-five horses at the time. He had about a dozen horses in training, five or six broodmares, and some yearlings. All of a sudden, Mike is thrown back into the Thoroughbred business. Ironically, the only stakes horse his dad ever had was at the time of his death. His name was Nickle Band, and he sort of gave Mike the taste for Thoroughbreds again. So while he was messing with Quarter Horses with me, he had these Thoroughbreds, some of which he had bought privately in partnership with Bob Roth, who lived up around Seattle.

My brother Bill had a restaurant in Seattle, and he got to know Bob Roth really well. Mike, who lived in Mt. Vernon, Washington, used to come in there with Bob, and they got a real kick out of Bill. Mike and Bob weren't doing too well with their horses, and they decided, "As long as we're losing, we might as well be with someone we can have fun with." Bob told Mike, "Wouldn't it be great if we could get Baffert to come in on the Thoroughbreds," and Mike said, "Yeah, that would be great."

Mike introduced me to Bob Roth over lunch. I had one Quarter Horse for them, one they had bought in partnership. He did okay, but he wasn't much. They asked me if I ever thought about switching over to Thoroughbreds. I was thinking that in order to do that, I needed a heavy-duty deal. I tried to come up with a number to throw at them, and I decided on $300,000, just to spook them pretty good. And they said, "Hell, we'll give you more than that. We've already blown a million, what's another $300,000?"

I told them what I needed to do was claim some horses first. The only way I was going to learn about the game was to claim horses and piddle around a little, just to get a feel for it and get my feet wet. I figured, after that, we'd go out and buy some horses. I just wanted to see what it was like before I plunged in there. I told them I didn't know what to expect, and that I had to re-train my mind all over. And they appreciated that.

I still kept my stable of Quarter Horses at Los Alamitos. In the summer of '88, I went to Del Mar to claim my first Thoroughbred. I put the claim in, and when the gates opened, the horse refused to come out. I was sick over it. When I got back there, I found out my claim was invalid. I had been so nervous filling out the form, I forgot to put the claiming price on. After the race, Mike asked me, "Did you claim that horse?" and I said, "No, I changed my mind at the last minute. The horse was acting weird and I felt something was fishy." I was too embarrassed to tell him what happened. So, I came out of it looking good. Mike was thinking, "Hey, this boy is okay, he's paying attention."

I was such an idiot, though. When I was driving down to Del Mar, I was so nervous, and I started thinking, "Oh my God, I don't have a Thoroughbred trainer's license." So when I arrived, I asked to go to the stewards because I needed to get a license in order to claim a horse in the fourth race. The guy told me it wasn't that easy, that I had to take a trainer's test first. Then, I just happened to mention I had a license at Los Alamitos, and he said, "Oh, well, you're okay. You already have a license." I felt like a damn moron. I didn't tell anybody that story, either.

Now I had to go out and find another horse to claim. I had met this girl who knew Thoroughbreds and she told me about this horse that she felt was worth claiming. She said it was a pretty good horse, so I went to look at him. His name was Hidden Royalty and he was trained by Brian Mayberry, who I didn't know from a hole in the wall. The Thoroughbred guys would put these paddock boots on their horses, and you couldn't see the horses' legs. When he came into the paddock, I thought he was a nice looking horse, so I put the claim in for $32,000. I was hoping he wouldn't win, because I wanted to claim a maiden who would run second or third, so I could run him back and break his maiden. I thought it would look good.

The horse wound up winning the race, going six furlongs in around 1:11, and it was an ugly win. He didn't run very fast and he was life and death. I went down to the track, and this one trainer asked me, "Who claimed the winner?" in a tone that sounded like, who was stupid enough to claim this horse. I told him, "I did." And he just looked at me and said, "Oh, okay."

That's when I met April Mayberry, Brian's daughter. We've been close ever since, and she does a great job running my stable at Churchill Downs. After the race, Brian said to April, "Go see who the dummy in the cowboy hat is who claimed my horse." She told him it was some Quarter Horse trainer named Bob Baffert. I remember seeing Terry Lipham afterward. Terry was a real good rider in his day, and had Eddie Delahoussaye's book at the time. He asked me what I was doing, and I told him I was claiming some horses and was thinking about switching over. He said, "Bob, let me tell you something. You're doing good; stay where you're at. This is too tough a game. I'm telling you, you can't make it over here."

Well, stuff like that really motivates me. I was determined to make it. I took Hidden Royalty back to the barn, and, I'll tell you, they named him right. He did have a hidden royalty — a broken splint bone. I think everyone on the backside knew he had it except me. I found a van and took him to my barn at Los Alamitos. On the way back, I called Mike and told him I claimed a horse from Brian Mayberry. He said, "Oh, it's a Siegel horse. It must be a nice horse." Mayberry trained privately for the Siegels — Jan, Mace, and their daughter Samantha — and they had a lot of good horses. I told Mike, "Yeah, he seems like a nice horse, but I think he needs to be gelded." The next day, I gelded him and gave him a week off, then started training him.

The first time I was going to work him, I was holding him at the gap, and I saw Alex Solis just standing around. Alex had ridden him when he broke his maiden. I was hoping to get his attention and ask him to work the horse for me. I saw his agent and asked him if Alex could work the horse a half-mile. If he liked him he could ride him back. If not, no big deal. He said, "Let me go ask him." He went over and asked him, and I could see them all looking over at me laughing. I was standing there with my cowboy hat on, and probably looked like some dumb shit to them. The agent came back and said, "Alex said he's too busy right now, and he doesn't want to ride him back anyway."

Meanwhile, I'm holding this horse, and he's spinning around in circles. I look at Alex, and he just walks off drinking his coffee. He had nothing else to do. He just left me there hanging with this sonofagun. I took him back to the barn and finally got an exercise rider to work him. I ran him back, and my brothers went out there, and he ran horribly. He got beat about ten lengths. I ran him again, and by the third time, my brothers didn't even bother coming. They'd tell me it was too far to drive.

I finally sent the horse to a friend of mine at Turf Paradise and told him to run him there for a $10,000 claiming tag. He ran there for ten, and I brought him back and ran him for twelve-five. He won, and was claimed.

The second horse I claimed was a different story. His name was Presidents Summit. What I did was go to a friend of mine, Bob Baedeker, who sold these clocker's tip sheets and I told him I needed some help. I said I really needed to claim a good horse for this new client, and he gave me this horse, Presidents Summit. I looked at the horse and he looked great. I had my assistant Tim Yakteen with me at the time and we went over and put the claim in for $50,000. I told Tim, "If this horse doesn't work out, I think I'm done in the Thoroughbred business. These guys aren't going to go for this deal." I just felt if this horse ran lousy I would lose all interest in Thoroughbreds.

I put in the claim and the horse comes from off the pace and wins. It was awesome. I felt like I had won the race. I'll never forget, I watched the race from behind the winner's circle, and afterward, everyone was telling me, "Hey, nice claim. Beautiful horse." I called Mike and told him I got a good one. I took him back and started my little one-horse stable. I ran him a couple times and he won again. It was really starting to get exciting.

During that time, I got another horse from Hal Earnhardt. He sent him to me from Arizona, and he won. Now things were starting to move along. I claimed a few others and piddled around, and the next year I told Mike I was ready to go to the sales.

I had gone to the sales once, right after I got involved with the Thoroughbreds in 1988. I still only had Hidden Royalty at the time, and I figured I'd go to the Keeneland fall yearling sales. Little did I know, with my one broken down claimer, that I'd return with a Breeders' Cup winner. R. D. Hubbard, the head of Hollywood Park, had asked me if I wanted to fly with him on his private jet. I had never been in a private jet before, and that was awesome. Meanwhile, Hal Earnhardt had told me if I saw a horse I really liked to go ahead and buy it. So I was looking for a horse for around fifteen or twenty grand. But every time I liked a horse he'd go for two hundred thousand. I said, "What the hell is going on here? This is crazy paying that kind of money for a horse."

Finally, after the third day, I saw this gray horse go through there, and this guy is beautiful. As he's going through there, I'm looking at him, and the girl tells me he's a ridgling. He's got one testicle up. I go, "Yes! All right!" I figured I'd get him cheaper. Bill Mitchell, the guy who owned Gold Coast Express was there, and he was looking to buy a few horses and pinhook them — sell them back the following year. While he was looking, I told him, "Bill, I just saw this beautiful gray sonofagun. You need to buy this horse." He agreed to buy him if he brought $20,000, but I told him he might bring more than that.

He went up to twenty-two, then twenty-five, and I told Bill to keep going, but he said it was too much. He told me, "You got other clients. If you like him that much, buy him for them." I remembered about Hal, so I hit him at thirty. But that was more than I usually spend for Hal. Once I made the bid, I said to myself, "Man, I hope someone ups the bid, so I can get out of this deal." Just then, I hear, "Sold, $30,000."

Now, I'm shaking like a leaf signing the ticket. As soon as I sign it, I jump up and take off to the barn. To show you how fast I got back there, I beat the horse. I'm back there and I run into this Quarter Horse trainer I know from Texas. I say to him, "What are you doing here?" He tells me he's trying to buy this horse and he thinks the owners just bought him back. They were looking for sixty, but bought him back for thirty. Just then, the gray horse comes walking in, and he says, "That's him there." I tell him, "Hell, I just bought this horse myself."

Now I'm still looking to get out of the deal, so I tell the guy,

"Look, if you like him, just give me a thousand bucks and I'll give you the ticket." Sometimes, if you want a horse and you miss it or you get there late, you can offer the buyer a thousand dollars and he'll give you the sales slip and you just go change the name. So, I offer this guy the horse, and he goes, "Nah, that's okay."

Now I got to sell this horse. I really wasn't too worried about it, but it was still mine until I sold it. I guess I could have gone to Mike, but all their money at the time was claiming money that was put into an account, and I didn't want to use up my claiming money. I called up Hal, and I made a mistake by leaving a message with his wife that I bought this horse for $30,000. She relayed it to him, and he called me back and told me it was too much money. He said he'd stay in for a piece if I wanted. But I told him not to worry about it. I'd get him sold.

Once again, this is why I believe in fate. I had gone to college with Jimmy Bell, from Jonabell Farm, and we became good friends. When we were in school, CB radios were really popular. I needed a handle for my CB, and Jimmy just happened to have a copy of *The Blood-Horse* magazine on his table. On the cover was a picture of a horse named Hatchet Man. I liked the name and told him I was going to be Hatchet Man. Even to this day, Jimmy still calls me Hatchet.

After the sale, I decided to go see Jimmy. I hadn't seen him in nine years. So I tore out the catalogue page on this colt, folded it up, and put it in my wallet. I went over to his barn, and his sister Bennie was there. She told me Jimmy was at the farm having a little party at the stallion barn, and asked if I wanted to go with her. I jumped in the car with Bennie and we went over there. Jimmy and I started talking, and he asked me if I bought anything. I told him I bought this one colt, and he asked me who he was by. I said, "I don't even know."

I pulled out the catalogue page and told him he's by a horse called Slewpy, but I had never heard of him. Jimmy says, "Well, turn around, and I'll introduce you to him." I just happened to be standing outside his stall, no more than a few feet from him. Jimmy then tells me, "I hope you have better luck than we've had. He's started off pretty slow." I thought that was pretty coincidental in itself, but then he asks what kind of mare he's out of. I look down at the page and I go, "Holy shit, he's out of a Hatchet Man mare." I tell him, "Hell, this has got to be a runner. Slewpy's here...Hatchet Man. This has to be a good horse." I started feeling much better about keeping him.

When I got back home, I contacted some of my old Quarter Horse people. I sold a third each to the Dutch Masters group of Dr. James Streelman and Denny Boer. I had once owned a horse in partnership with Mitch DeGroot, my friend from the Quarter Horses whose wife was killed in a training accident. I owed Mitch five thousand dollars and I asked him if he wanted to take half of my third and call it even, and he agreed.

When I told Mike what had happened, he said, "Why didn't you just tell me? I would have taken the horse." I told him I didn't want to use my claiming money, and he said he would have put more money in. As it turned out, the ownership of the horse changed quite a bit, and Mike would come in later. By the time it was all straightened out, Mitch DeGroot owned a third, Doc Streelman owned a third, and Denny Boer and Mike Pegram each owned a half of a third.

At the time, the Thoroughbreds were a losing deal, and it was the Quarter Horses that were keeping me afloat. But it was only a matter of time when this gray colt named Thirty Slews would put me on the map.

THE BIG SWITCH

"I started out as Bob's personal slave. He gave me the worst jobs imaginable. The only thing he didn't do was send a pack of wild dogs after my ass. Let's just say he did everything he could to try to break me, but I wouldn't give up. I knew when I had a good thing and I wasn't about to let it go. There was no room for error. Bob had zero tolerance when it came to me and he bore down on me relentlessly, because he knew that was the only way I was going to learn, and I appreciated that. The reason I stuck it out with Bob was that I could see right away that he was a winner. And a winner is a winner no matter what business you're in. One motto Bob has always lived by is, 'A happy staff does a great job.' And as tough as he was on me, he always made it a fun place to work. I'll never forget the one night after he won a stakes at Los Alamitos on Halloween night, he showed up in the winner's circle wearing a pumpkin head. All I know is that if I were a flower, I'd have Bob to thank for helping me blossom into what I am."

— Assistant trainer Tim Yakteen

Thirty Slews was late coming around and didn't get to the races until he was three in 1990. Early that year, I decided it was time to go to the two-year-old sales and look for some horses for Mike and Bob, who raced under the name Romi Stables, short for Robert and Mike.

We went to a two-year-olds in training sale in Ocala, and I bought Broadway's Top Gun for $80,000. He went on to become our first stakes

119

winner, taking the Phoenix Futurity at Turf Paradise and Ladbroke Futurity at Golden Gate later that year. The following year, he won the Bolsa Chica at Santa Anita and placed in several other stakes.

We didn't realize how close we had already come to having a major star. In 1989, we went to the Super Bowl in Miami, then paid a visit to Clyde Rice's farm to look at some horses. Clyde tried to sell me this horse for $100,000. He looked okay, but I felt it was way too much money for a horse off the farm. Bob Roth really wanted the horse, but I told him he was too light. I was used to these muscular Quarter Horses.

A year later, Clyde Rice came up to me and said, "Hey Bob, you should have bought that horse I tried to sell you guys." I said, "Why, did he turn out all right?" And he said, "Yeah, as a matter of fact, he runs up there in California. You might know him." I asked him what his name was and he said Farma Way. I go, "Oh shit. Don't tell that to Mike and Bob, whatever you do." Farma Way wound up going to Lukas, and he won the Santa Anita Handicap and Pimlico Special and earned almost $3,000,000.

By 1990, I still had sixty Quarter Horses, but only two or three Thoroughbreds. Eventually, John Bassett sent me some Thoroughbreds who had gotten too good for the Arizona circuit, and they turned out to be nice horses. When I had left Arizona, I gave my top Quarter Horse clients to John, and they had some pretty nice Thoroughbreds as well. There was Soviet Sojourn, owned by Hal Earnhardt, who would become the dam of Indian Charlie. She won the Junior Miss and Sorrento at Del Mar in 1991 and placed in the Del Mar Debutante, Oak Leaf, and Hollywood Starlet. Bassett also sent me a gelding named Gundaghia, owned and bred by Bob Kieckhefer, who is my oldest client, and some partners. He was a tough old horse who won stakes on turf and dirt. A couple of other stakes horses Bassett sent me were First Intent and Viva El Capitan. I finally got Thirty Slews to the races in the winter of '90. I had decided to bring him around slowly. Right after I bought him, I sent him straight to Los Alamitos. I had even tried to sell him to R. D. Hubbard on the plane going home. He had just spent over a million dollars at the sale, and I told him I had this real nice horse I bought, and that I was stuck with him. I asked him if he wanted to go half on the horse or buy all of him. He looked up the horse's pedigree and checked what Slewpy had done, and said, "Sorry, Baffert, you're on your own on this one."

When I got him home, one of my assistants, Laura Pinelli, who is now married to Wayne Lukas, said, "What's the matter with his head? He's got some big indentation." I didn't notice that when I bought him. At first I was worried he had a caved-in skull or something, but I guess they get that from laying in their stall.

I would have kept the horse for myself, but Sherry and I were looking to buy a house at the time. When Laura asked me what I paid for him, I said, "Thirty freakin' slews." That's how he got his name. I sent him to a Quarter Horse ranch to be broken, and when I got him to the track the following winter, I started breezing him a little. I had Kip Didericksen breeze him a quarter of a mile one morning. When he came back, I asked him what he thought, and he said, "You must own this horse yourself." I asked him why he thought that, and he said, "Because he's not very fast."

He was a big horse and just wasn't that quick when he was young. Also, because he was a ridgling, his testicle was bothering him. He wasn't putting out, so I sent him to a vet and had him castrated. At the time, I didn't know that you could cut out the one little one and leave the one big one. I brought him back and started training him again. I only had a few stalls at Los Alamitos, and I needed them for my other horses. I knew this guy, and he told me to send Thirty Slews down to Tijuana with his trainer Pepe Magana, and he'd train him for me for twenty bucks a day. Pepe was a real good horse-man, so I sent him to Tijuana to save some money, and he was down there training for about a month. Then one day, Pepe calls me up and says, "Hey, Bob, this big gray horse is a runnin' sonofabitch. He's way too much horse for down here. You got to get him out of here."

After I got Thirty Slews back, I sent him to Del Mar to work him three-eighths. They stabled me in the worst barn on the backstretch. They called it the chicken barn, because that's where they kept all the poultry during the fair. They had these portable stalls put up, and this big horse barely fit in them. One day, he rubbed up against the side, and the whole damn thing collapsed.

I worked him three-eighths and just told the rider to let me see what he's got. He worked in :33⅗ and looked like he was galloping. When he got back, he was blowing hard and looked a little tight in the shoulders, like he had done something down below. We scanned his leg, and he had this tiny hole in his tendon, the size of a pin-head. The vet said to give him a few months off and he'd be okay. So I blistered him and turned him out for four months.

I brought him back and got him ready to run that winter. The first time I ran him he won by three and a half lengths and he looked awesome. R. D. Hubbard came down to the winner's circle after the race to congratulate me. He said, "This isn't that same sonofabitch you bought at that sale when I gave you the ride, is it?" I told him this was the horse, and he said, "That figures." I had known Hubbard since 1982 when I was training Quarter Horses at Rillito and was always pretty tight with him. But our friendship sort of went sour when this group of trainers convinced me to go on strike with them after he took over Hollywood Park.

I ran Thirty Slews back and he won again, and that's when I got my first taste of Derby fever. It was amazing. I sent him to Keeneland for the Lexington Stakes, and Jimmy Bell set me up in Sam Ramer's barn. I came in there so excited. I really felt like I was going good now. Here I'm just getting started and I'm one race away from the Kentucky Derby. Mike hadn't come in on the horse yet, but he went with me anyway. One thing about Mike, he loves road trips.

After we got there, I wanted to work him five-eighths, and I told the girl he wasn't a very good work horse, so if she saw another horse breaking off in front of him, that would be okay. The track was really heavy that day, and she took off after this other horse. Well, he wound up working way too fast. They got him in :57⅘. One of the clockers yelled to me from the stand, "Hey, is that your horse? I've been here for twenty years and I've never seen a horse work that fast."

I actually got all excited when I heard that. But then I watched him come off the track and he was coughing and gagging. I mean he was one tired puppy. Even back at the barn, this poor sonofagun was blowing hard. After that, he was real quiet the rest of the week. I cooked him right then, and he never got back on his toes.

While I was there, ESPN came in and wanted to do a feature on me. They wanted to compare me with Wayne Lukas, because we had both come up through the Quarter Horses. So, they tried to portray me as the next Wayne Lukas. I told them, "I don't think so." One of the questions they asked me was, "How long have you known Wayne Lukas?" And I said, "Hell, I knew Wayne when he had bad teeth." Well, everybody started to crack up. I guess that was my first shining moment with the media.

I ran Thirty Slews in the Lexington, and he went to the lead. By the time he turned for home he was dead. That poor horse showed so much guts to finish third. When he got back to the barn, he was nothing but hair and lactic acid. He started breathing funny, so we scoped him, and his flapper, or epiglottis, was paralyzed a little bit.

He was really messed up. Not only was it disappointing to lose the race, but my dreams of going to the Kentucky Derby suddenly were dead. When I realized I didn't have a Derby horse, it was devastating. I was totally bummed out.

So I packed up and sent him home and brought him back to the races in late June, and he won an allowance race at Hollywood by five lengths in 1:08⅘. But he was still having breathing problems, and he had a problem with an ankle. I ran him in the Vernon Underwood in November and he stopped like a shot, so I wound up putting him away for nine months.

The following year, 1991, I met Bob Lewis. I happened to be hanging around Clocker's Corner one morning and he came up to me and introduced himself. He said, "By any chance, are you any relation to Melissa Baffert from Nogales?" I told him she was my cousin. As it turned out, Melissa had gone to school with Bob's daughter Nancy and they were close friends. So we got to talking, and he told me how he used to have a Porsche dealership in Tucson, and I told him I remembered it. At the time, he was just getting involved in Thoroughbreds, and he had a private trainer. About an hour later, he came walking by my barn and said, "Bob, I just want you to know that I have a private trainer named Frank Vega, who's a very nice fellow. But I enjoyed talking to you, and I'd like to leave you my card. If you ever find me a horse, give me call. I'd like to have a horse with you."

I was all excited, but I never did find a horse for him. I looked, but I just couldn't find the right kind of horse. That September, I was at the Keeneland sale, and Bob was there looking for horses. I had this Cal-bred named Ebonair who had just broken his maiden at Del Mar, and he was a pretty nice horse that I had bought for this other client of mine for fourteen grand. The first time I ran him I thought he couldn't lose. I was out of town at the time, and I called my assistant and said, "I can't believe he got beat. Who the hell beat him?" And my assistant said, "Some horse called Bertrando."

I ran Ebonair back two weeks later, and I was watching the race on TV at Keeneland. I told Bob Lewis that I have this good horse, and the owner wants to sell him. I asked Bob to come watch him run. I told him the owner wanted a hundred grand, and he might be worth the money if he ran well. The horse won in 1:09 and change and looked great. So I bought the horse for Bob, and I ran him back in a stakes and he ran second. Then, I put him in the Cal Cup Juvenile and he won. That was Bob Lewis' first hundred grander.

After the race, Bob told me he wanted to go to the Keeneland July sales, and that he was looking to spend two million dollars. I'm going, "Sonofabitch." But I kept my cool, and I told him, "Sure, okay." But this was October, and there was too much time in between. By the time the July sale came around, I told Bob I would feel better if he waited for the September sale. I felt we'd get better value. He said okay, but shortly after that he met John T. L. Jones of Walmac International and bloodstock agent John Moynihan, and they bought him a few horses at the July sale.

My problem was that I just wasn't ready to spend his money. It was the same when I had first met Mike. I've always been the kind of guy who wanted to get a feel for something first. And I wanted to get a feel for the yearling sales before I spent that kind of money. I didn't want to go there and blow two million bucks and not come back with good horses. I just wasn't ready for it. I did manage to buy Bob one horse for two hundred grand named Sir Hutch, and he turned out to be a good horse. But I really blew it, because Bob was dying to get into it heavy at that point. He picked up some other trainers that year and gave them horses.

That same year, 1991, my assistant Tim Yakteen left to go to work for Charlie Whittingham. He didn't want to leave, but I told him this was an opportunity to work for one of the greatest trainers that ever lived. I said he'd better go with Charlie, because I didn't know how far I was going to go with Thoroughbreds. And believe it or not, Charlie actually came over to me and asked me for my permission to hire Tim. I don't know any trainer who would do that.

I knew Charlie was a great trainer of turf horses, so I told Tim if Charlie asked him what experience he had with turf horses, don't tell him that the only turf experience we ever had was when one of our horses got loose and jumped over the rail and ran loose on the turf course.

I'll never forget the day I hired Tim at Los Alamitos in 1987. He had never ridden horses, and had actually rented a horse from a riding stable with his girlfriend. He was paying rent just to work with the horse and ride a little bit. When he came to me, I asked him if he could ride, and he said, "Yeah, I can ride." I asked him how long he had been riding. He started thinking, and said "Well, I've been riding since..." I was expecting him say since he was a little kid. He pauses and says, "I've been riding since Thanksgiving." Well, I just about fell off my chair. I said, "You got the job."

Holly Golightly was my assistant at the time, and I told her, "We'll put him in charge of leading the horses back and forth to the track." That's the worst job there is. You're talking about twenty-five or thirty trips to and from the barn every day. I said to her, "Believe me, after a week, he won't want to be a trainer." But this guy turned out to be a working sonofagun. I started him grooming horses and he worked his way up. Now, he's made full circle. When Charlie was in bad health before he died and didn't need him anymore, Tim came back to me.

There's one story about Tim I tell whenever we all want a good laugh. He had been working for me for only six months or so, and I had him grooming this horse named Zip Into Cash, owned by Dutch Masters, who I decided to send down to Arizona for the Sonoita Futurity. When I was growing up, the Sonoita Futurity was the main race. That was our first Saturday in May. When I was at Los Alamitos, I would send a horse down there to run in it every year. I'd send him for the trials first, then leave him there with my dad. He'd take care of him and put him on the hot-walking machine, then haul him up there and run him. You really didn't have to do much with Quarter Horses. They were always fit.

I usually sent Holly with the horse, but she couldn't go this particular year, so I got Tim, even though he still was really green. I told Tim this would be a great experience for him. He'd get down there for the trials, then my baby brother Gamble would bring him back to the ranch to stay. I called my mom and told her I was sending a groom down to stay with her named Haitham Yakteen, which is Tim's real name. He's half German and half Arab. My mother wasn't too thrilled about having to put up one of my grooms. She didn't know what the hell to expect. She pictured some low-life with missing teeth.

I assured her he was a very, very nice guy who was low maintenance, and he was just going to be taking care of the horse. No one knew he had just started working for me. So Tim buys himself a cowboy hat and goes down to the farm. Meanwhile, my mom's still bitching about having to take care of this groom. After Tim arrives, I call him and he fills me in on everything in great detail. One thing about Tim, he's the most conscientious person who's ever worked for me. Then my dad gets on and he says, "Don't worry. Everything's good here."

That night, Tim, Gamble, and my mom and dad went out to dinner. When they came back, I spoke to my mom and said I hoped Tim wasn't too much trouble. She said, "Oh, I just love him. What a nice young man."

When it was time for the trials, I flew into Tucson and went home to spend the night in Nogales. The next morning we went to Sonoita to run the horse. Tim and I loaded him in my dad's two-horse trailer and drove to the track. Holly Golightly was now working with her husband, John, as private trainer for Hal Earnhardt in Arizona, and they were stabled next to us. The horses were stabled in these metal port-o-stable barns, and John and Holly got a nice stall ready for the horse.

Whenever I showed up down there, all the local trainers would gather round to see what the big hot dog California trainer was bringing. I had won this race twice before. I told Tim, "Okay, here's what we're gonna do. I'm gonna open up the back of the van and you unhook him in the front." There was a front door and an escape door on the side where a person can climb out. I said to him, "You let me know when you have him unhooked and I'll open up the back, then we'll back him out." Meanwhile, all these trainers are watching us.

We walk up there like big shots and I open up the back. But Tim opens up the side door, and all of a sudden the horse sticks his head out the door and starts to crawl out the side of the trailer through an opening that is just big enough for a human. Tim screams my name, and I yell, "Oh shit!" I know that if the horse tries to squeeze through there he's going to tear his legs apart. He's got his head out, and I'm trying to push him back. Just then, somebody comes along and takes his hat and hits him over the head with it. The horse ducks his head and takes a big old chunk of hair and flesh off his head above the ears. He runs off the back of the trailer and I catch him. Now the horse is shaking his head around and I'm dying of embarrassment, because everyone is watching all this and laughing.

I start to walk the horse around and he's mad as hell and still shaking his head around, with a big chunk of skin missing. I bring him in the barn and put him in the stall, and I say to Tim, "What the hell happened to you? I never told you to open the side door. Man, you embarrassed the shit out of me. This could have been a disaster." Tim is all flustered and he starts apologizing. I tell him, "Whatever you do, don't leave the halter on this horse after you leave the stall. Take it off when you're done, because he can catch the halter on the hooks near the outside of the stall and hang up his head." Tim says, "Don't worry, Bob, no more mistakes."

A few minutes before we're about to go the paddock, Tim goes in the horse's stall to grease his feet up. Holly is holding the horse while he's greasing his feet, and I'm standing about a hundred feet away, talking to my dad. Tim then turns the horse loose in the stall after he's done greasing him up and forgets to take the halter off. All of a sudden, I hear all this commotion in the stall. I look over and the horse's head is hung up on one of the hooks. This poor horse is banging his head on the side of this metal wall and all this sawdust is flying all over the place. The next thing I know, the horse's head has disappeared, but the halter is still hanging on the hook. The horse had come out of his halter, and I go running over there screaming, "Jesus Christ, what did you do?"

Now the poor horse's skin is torn completely off the back of his ears and he's really pissed. He's stomping the ground and throwing his head around. I yell to Tim, "Leave this horse alone and get the hell out of there. Don't get near this sonofabitch. You're gonna kill him. Not only are you gonna kill this horse, you're gonna kill me." Tim wants to help, but I say, "No! The last thing this horse wants to see is you in his stall. Just let him cool off. As soon as it looks like he's calmed down we'll go in there and brush him off, put the bridle on him and walk him up there." By now, poor Tim is a nervous wreck.

My dad is watching all this and he asks me what the hell is going on. He didn't even see the trailer incident. We take the horse over for the trials and he wins his heat and qualifies about fifth fastest for the finals. So we load him back in the trailer and drive him back to Nogales. I tell Tim, "You know, I'm gonna send you back with me. I need you back in California. I'm gonna leave the horse with The Chief. He knows what to do." I go up to the house and my dad is lying on his bed watching TV. He says to me, "By the way, Bob, I want to ask you something. This Tim, how long has he worked for you?" I tell him just a few months. He says, "He seems a little green." I tell him, "Green? He knows nothing. I'm just teaching him." My father starts screaming, "Jesus Christ! No wonder. I didn't want to say anything."

I tell him I'm taking Tim home with me and leaving him in charge. Just then, Tim walks in and tells my dad he's leaving with me and that he left everything out for him. He starts telling him about the feed, and before he can get another word out, my dad goes, "Tim, F___ you! I'm taking over the show! Jesus, I thought you knew what the hell you were doing." We all start cracking up laughing. I'll say this for Tim, he had my dad fooled for a week. As it turned out, my dad hauled the horse up there for me and he won the finals.

After Tim left to join Whittingham, I hired a guy who had worked for Dick Mandella and he stayed with me for about a year. John Russell knew I was looking for an assistant, and he came up to me and said he was down on horses, and that he had this really good kid named Eoin Harty. I said to tell him to come by the barn. I had always seen Eoin on the pony when he worked with Russell, and he always looked like some nerdy guy with glasses. I used to call him Mr. Peabody, after the cartoon character. But once I started talking to him, I saw that he was very sharp, and a funny guy. He's been my number one guy ever since.

The fall of '91 was a major turning point in my life. I still had a large stable of Quarter Horses at Los Alamitos, but I was thinking of getting rid of them. I sent two horses — Ed Grimley and Holland Ease — to another trainer to prepare them for the All American Futurity at Ruidoso. I had never run a horse in the All American before. I would have taken them myself, but I had Soviet Sojourn running really well at Del Mar. I look back now and I wish I would have taken them. Ed Grimley was a real fast, talented horse and I think I could have won the All American with him had I been with the horse. I told this guy to run the two horses through the trials and I'd split the stakes with him.

I called up Mike, and I told him, "Why don't you go to Ruidoso with me? This is my last hurrah in Quarter Horses. We'll fly to El Paso, drive to the track for the race, then come back." Mike said, "You know what? Let's go out in style. We'll charter a plane, take the guys with us, and make a party out of it."

I got us a Lear jet, and it was me, Mike, Bill, P. A., and my vet, Vince Baker, who was also like one of my brothers. He went everywhere with us. Mitch DeGroot, who owned and bred Ed Grimley, reserved us a three-bedroom condo, and everything was set. Well, the first thing that went wrong was that there was no bathroom on the plane and everyone was doing some serious beer drinking. Meanwhile, the pilot was just circling around, and we were convinced he was lost. As it turned out, I think they had moved the airport at Ruidoso and he was trying to find it.

Bill couldn't hold it in any longer, so he peed in his empty beer can. Before long, we were all peeing in the trash cans. As soon as the plane landed and they opened the doors, everyone started peeing right on the runway. You would have thought the radiator had a hole in it. I had gone to see if I could get a car, and when I got back it looked like the plane had been leaking fuel, there was such a big puddle under it.

I hadn't bothered to arrange for a car, because I thought the airport would have a rent-a-car booth, but there was nothing. The driver who had come to pick up the pilots had this old Chevy Impala, so we all jumped in with them. We went to the condo and they told us they had already rented it. We were late, and no one had bothered to guarantee it with a credit card number.

Here we arrive in a Lear jet to run two horses in a million-dollar race, and we drive up with seven of us packed in an old Chevy Impala and have no hotel room. We drove to the Inn of the Mountain Gods, the only decent hotel in town, and they didn't have anything. Bill was in the hotel business, and he talked to the girl about getting something for us. He said we'd take anything they had. She said all they had was one of the conference rooms, and they could bring in some roll-a-way beds. We said we'll take it. The room smelled of smoke, and when you turned the lights on, you could have gotten a sun tan, it was so bright. But it did have a bathroom.

That night, they had the All American Ball, which we called the Hayseed Ball, because everyone wore cowboy hats. We had no way of getting there without a car, so we took one of the trash cans, filled it with ice and beer, then went down and paid the bellman a hundred bucks to drive us to the party in the hotel's courtesy van. We wound up keeping the van for the whole weekend, making sure the trash can was filled with beer at all times. They quit serving liquor at twelve o'clock in New Mexico, but the van driver had a friend who worked in a convenience store, and he sold us beer out of the back room.

In the All American, Ed Grimley went off as the favorite and got beat a neck, and Holland Ease ran fourth. We were pissed. We flew out of there after the race and returned to Del Mar. A short time later, on Cal Cup Day 1991, I got rid of my Quarter Horses. And ironically, on that day, I won three Cal Cup races. I had been reluctant to give up my Quarter Horses, but I was talking to Lukas in the paddock one day. He asked me if I still had the Quarter Horses, and I told him I did, and that it was tough running both stables. He said, "Let me tell you something. Get rid of them. I was the same way. I didn't want to get rid of them. But the minute I did, my business tripled."

A month later, I won the three Cal Cup races — with Ebonair, Letthebighossroll, and Charmonnier, and almost won a fourth. Charmonnier's win was a big upset, as he beat Best Pal, one of the best horses of the decade. Best Pal had finished second in the Kentucky Derby that year and beat older horses in the first Pacific Classic. I really drilled Charmonnier, and I knew Best Pal's trainer Gary Jones wasn't really pointing the horse for that race. When he won, I was thrilled, because it showed I could train a horse to go two turns.

Later that night, Los Alamitos had their big night of stakes. It was like their Breeders' Cup. I went down there and told everybody this was my last night in the Quarter Horse business. I'm quitting right after the races. And would you believe, the last Quarter Horse race I won was the last race of the night, and I won it with a son of Five OClock Rush, the horse whose nose victory kept me from packing up and going back to Arizona.

BREEDERS' CUP AND BEYOND

"Bob can be a jerk, but you've got to love the guy. He's a lot smarter than most people give him credit for. They take him at face value and only go by that goofing off attitude of his, and it rubs them the wrong way. But he's got a memory like an elephant. He remembers every damn thing about a horse, from what they looked like as a yearling to their pedigree to the equipment they wear in the paddock. He can treat people like shit at times, but he does respect your opinion and he makes things fun. I used to work for a real hard-nosed guy for five years, and when I was looking for work I was offered jobs by two trainers who had far better horses than Bob. But after talking to Bob, I thought, 'What the hell, even if it doesn't work out, at least I'll have fun for six months.' I feel blessed to have this job, and I thank God every day I've got it. It's been great seeing Bob go from 'Mr. Cal-bred' to 'Mr. Sprinter' to 'Mr. Derby.'" — *Assistant trainer Eoin Harty*

Thirty Slews continued to have breathing problems and ankle problems throughout his four-year-old campaign in 1991, and I was only able to start him four times. He spent more time on the farm than he did at the track. He just barely won an allowance race on the Hollywood turf course going five and a half furlongs and he was second in the Bing Crosby at Del Mar and the Underwood at Hollywood Park. He was always making this whistling noise, and his flapper kept getting paralyzed.

In January of 1992, I ran him down the hill on the Santa Anita turf course and he got beat a dozen lengths. Then he ran badly again in the El Conejo. He just couldn't breathe any longer, so I thought about running him for a $50,000 claiming tag and getting rid of him. Then my vet, Vince Baker, suggested we send him to Dr. Wayne McIlwraith to do a tie-back surgery, where they tie back the flapper. Most of them don't work, so I wasn't expecting much. They performed the surgery, and when I got him back, he started training awesome again. He finally could breathe. He had always run great fresh, so I ran him in the Bing Crosby off a five and a half-month layoff and he blew by horses in the stretch to win by about two lengths in 1:08⅕.

I was on a roll at that time, and I went to Mike and told him, "I don't know how I can thank you for getting me in the Thoroughbreds. It's changed my life and I want to do something to repay you." So I gave him my piece of Thirty Slews, and that's how he became part-owner of the horse.

I ran him back in a small stakes at Del Mar, coupled with Gundaghia. Eddie Delahoussaye was on Thirty Slews and Gary Stevens was on Gundaghia. I told Gary his only shot was to steal away turning for home. But at the eighth pole, if he started to hear the theme song from *Jaws*, not to panic. That'll be Thirty Slews coming up behind him. Sure enough, turning for home, Gundaghia looked like he was home free, and Thirty Slews started coming after him. But he really had to work hard, and just got up in the last few jumps to win.

Mike couldn't come for the race, and when he asked me what I thought, I told him I was going to run one-two. He had me bet a $2,000, one-way exacta, Thirty Slews to Gundaghia. Coming down the stretch, I was rooting for Thirty Slews to catch him, and when they asked me why I was pulling for one horse over other, I told them I was rooting for Mike's exacta.

After that race, I started thinking about running him in the

Breeders' Cup Sprint at Gulfstream, but they told me I might not have enough points based on stakes earnings to get in. I figured I'd still take a chance. I decided I was going to train him up to the race, which was about two months away, and just go for broke. It was the same thing I did with Gold Coast Express in the Champion of Champions. As it turned out, he didn't have enough points, but luckily he got invited.

He was 5-2 at Santa Anita and about 80-1 in New York. He wound up going off at 18-1 at Gulfstream. He trained so awesome for the race, I knew he was going to run big. I worked him three-quarters in 1:10 before I shipped him to Florida. But I didn't want the same thing to happen that happened in the Lexington Stakes, so I gave him a real easy five-furlong work, and he went in 1:03. I actually wanted him to go in about 1:01. Rubiano, the favorite for the race, broke off well behind him in the work and almost caught him. When the rider came back, I told him I wanted him to go faster than that, but I figured I'd make it up by picking up his gallops. One thing I've learned, you can never make up for a fast work, but you can always make up for a slow work the rest of the week.

Thirty Slews was a bad bleeder, so five days before he ran, I treated him with Lasix, a diuretic, and Robinul, a therapeutic drug that helps dry out the bronchial passages. There were no vets around because the meet hadn't opened yet, and I didn't know what to expect, so I brought my own stuff. There was no problem giving him Robinul, because it clears out of the system in a couple of days.

I'm very careful with this drug, because I had had a positive for it back in 1991, a month and a half before I won the three Cal Cup races. I had given it to one of my horses, a maiden $32,000 claimer, through a nebulizer to clear up his mucus. A lot of guys were using it, so we didn't think it would be a problem. However, they wound up slapping me with a two-week suspension. I was going to try to beat it, but it would have cost me around twenty grand, and my lawyer suggested I just take a two-week vacation. I hadn't taken a vacation for five years, so I took Sherry to Hawaii for one week and went to the Calder sales the other week. Rumors had started that I had given my three Cal Cup winners something. I vowed right then and there, I would never help one of these horses out like that again. It always seems to happen with the cheap ones. I told the investigators after it was over, "Boys, that's the last shot you'll ever get at me."

I get to the tack room at ten o'clock, the night before Thirty Slews' work, and I bring everything with me, because there are no vets at the track at four in the morning, when we have to administer the Lasix. While I'm mixing it, the guy I had with me, named Jake, is reading the pamphlet that comes with the medication. He starts reading it out loud, "Side effects: May cause two weeks in Hawaii." We just broke up laughing.

After that Robinul incident, it seemed as if every time I started winning races, people thought I had to be using something, especially coming from the Quarter Horses. I'll tell you, though, when you get a positive and get suspended, it's the most embarrassing and humiliating situation.

I tried to tell everyone how awesome Thirty Slews was doing, but no one knew who the hell I was and they really didn't care. The morning of the race, I started to put a tie on, but I decided I wasn't going to wear a tie, because they were bad luck. I went to get Mike in his room, and when I opened the door, I looked at him and he's got shorts on. He's going to the Breeders' Cup and he's wearing shorts. I said to him, "Mike, you can't wear shorts." He said, "Why not, it's hot out there?" I told him, "First of all, they won't let you in the paddock; and second, it's the Breeders' Cup, you got to dress up. Go put your jeans on." We both realized what I had said, and we cracked up laughing. So he went back and put on jeans and a sports jacket, and that's why you never see Mike in anything but jeans for a big race. We all went out there and we bet a bundle on the horse.

It turned out to be a two-horse race. The three-year-old filly Meafara busted out of there and we sat right in behind her. Passing the eighth pole, she opened up on him by over two lengths, but that old horse just kept digging. Delahoussaye rode him for all he was worth, and he just wore her down to win by a neck. Rubiano closed ground late, but he never got near them. When they hit the wire, I felt the same way I did with Gold Coast Express. I thought, "It's not going to get any better than this. This is it. I've hit the top of my profession."

They had a real bad spill in the race and I didn't even know it happened. The English colt, Mr Brooks, went down at the quarter pole, and I didn't find out about it until an hour later. One good thing about winning the first of the Breeders' Cup races, you get to enjoy the rest of the day. I was with Mike and Mitch DeGroot and some girls they had with them, and we did some heavy-duty drinking after the race. At the end of the day, about eight o'clock, I went to get the car, and told them I'd meet them back at the barn. I didn't know they had races the next day, so I started driving on the track. A security guard saw me and told me to get off there. I noticed some lights by the eighth pole, and there was some shit going on there. I saw Mike and Mitch and the girls walking back from there and they were all laughing.

What had happened was that Mike had lifted this girl up on the rail and started making out big-time with her. Just then, a security guard showed up and started flashing his lights on them. Mike threw his hands up in the air and yelled to the guard, "You got me." Mike told him he had won the Breeders' Cup Sprint and that they were just having a little fun. The guard just told them to get the hell out of there. Mike wound up naming a horse Loveontherail after that incident.

What was strange about winning the Breeders' Cup was that the race didn't do anything for my career. I still was known only as a sprint trainer, and it didn't get me any new clients. No one really cared that I had won a Breeders' Cup race.

Thirty Slews was never the same after the race. He wrenched his ankle a little bit and I gave him plenty of time afterward, but he never trained like he did before the Breeders' Cup. He ran for two more seasons, starting seven times with three seconds and one third. I ran him in the Breeders' Cup Sprint the following year, and he finished fourth, beaten two lengths. If I knew then what I know now, I think I could have won three Breeders' Cups with him. I trained him too hard, and I wound up learning a lot from that. There's an expression which goes, "A good horse is like a loaded gun. It's dangerous in anyone's hands." Well, my training of Thirty Slews was a perfect example of that. I only won that race because I got lucky.

Another thing I learned in those first three years after coming over from the Quarter Horses, in Quarter Horses all the big money is in the two-year-old races — all those futurities. The older they get the less money they run for. So, you had to have your horses ready early and keep them running all through their two-year-old campaign. But with Thoroughbreds, I noticed there were a lot of horses I hurt, because they'd get a little shin problem and I'd keep going. I'd train on them so hard, they'd wind up cracking their shin and I would have to put screws in them. It took me a few years, but I finally realized that if these horses were going to last, I had to get rid of that Quarter Horse mentality. When you turn them out and bring them back, the money is still going to be there.

By now, racing had become my entire life — seven days a week, with little time for anything else. Ever since I came to California in '83, it was like I was always climbing to get to the top. Then when I did get there, I realized you cannot back off at all. I tried to spend more time with my family, but it became more and more difficult.

By the end of '92, I had several owners, with about a third of the stable owned by Mike Pegram and Bob Roth. My owners Bob and Barbara Walter of Northern California, who owned and bred Charmonnier, took their horses away from me after I ran Charmonnier in the Strub Series and he didn't do any good. Mr. Walter decided to send the horses home after that, and he never sent them back to me. They all went to different trainers.

Charmonnier had a quarter crack in the back and we didn't do any good after the Cal Cup. I was a little upset that they fired me. I didn't think they should have, but they did. They had a ranch manager who wanted to train horses himself, and I think I was getting a lot of gas poured on me at the time. Their horses were all home-breds, so it wasn't like I had picked them out myself. If I had, it would have bothered me a lot more. But I don't believe in burning my bridges, and I was lucky I didn't in this case, because several years later, the Walters would send me horses again, including Cavonnier.

Over the next few years, I had a few little stakes horses, but I was kind of discouraged that winning the Breeders' Cup did so little for my career. It didn't help me at all. I was still buying a few horses, but the years after the Breeders' Cup were kind of dead. Bob Lewis wound up hitting it off with Wayne Lukas during that time, and I was thinking I had really missed the boat on that deal. What made it even worse was that I had stepped in and helped bring them together.

Lukas wasn't doing that well at the time, and he asked me one day why Bob Lewis had so many different trainers. I told him he was a real nice guy, and if you were nice to him and he liked you, he'd give you a horse. Wayne had spoken to Bob once, and Bob really didn't like his attitude. At the time, I felt like I was completely out with

Bob, because I really hadn't done much for him, and he was getting strong with Ray and Tom Bell. I had no momentum at all with Bob, and I didn't want to bug him. He gave me a few horses now and then, but I could tell we were going nowhere. So when I spoke to Wayne, I told him about the way Bob felt, and he went right in there, and the next thing I knew, they were taking off together.

I also learned a lot from that experience. Wayne had talked to Bob about giving him a three-year plan. That's when I learned that you can't do anything in one year; it takes three years to really get the ball rolling. If you get lucky after three years and buy the right kind of horses, they should start paying for themselves.

In 1995, I was at the Barretts two-year-old sale. I was talking to my insurance man Hal Oliver and he said a friend of his, Bob Walter, would like to send me some horses. I was doing pretty good at the time, winning some stakes, but I didn't have any big horses. I told Hal, "Forget about it. No way. They fired me once and I don't want to have anything to do with it." Hal said, "I'm telling you, Bob. I was up there and they've got some really good-looking horses. They're Cal-breds and you don't have any Cal-breds. Just talk to the guy. He's really okay."

Del Mar was coming up, and I said to Hal, "Okay, have him call me. He's going to have to call me." Shortly after, I got a call from Bob Walter and he said he wanted to send me some horses if I had the room. I said I didn't have that much room because we were about to go to Del Mar, and I told him to just send me the best ones. So, he sent me two horses — Batroyale and Argonnier.

I remember with Batroyale, after I got her, I brought her to Del Mar and galloped her a few times and was going to work her five-eighths. She was such a huge filly, all the time I was thinking she was a three-year-old. So I worked her with a three-year-old and she goes in :58 and change with Gary Stevens up and beats the other horse by a couple of lengths. I hadn't gotten her papers yet, and all Mr. Walter told me was that she had had a few starts and should get better as she got older. I told Eoin this filly can run and that maybe we can find a non-winners of three other than for her. Her papers had just come in and I was on the radio, so I told Eoin to go check and see how many races she'd won. He called me back, and he said, "Bob, this filly isn't three, she's two." I couldn't believe it.

There happened to be a two-year-old filly stakes — the Sorrento — closing that day and I put her in and got Stevens to ride. She won pretty easily, then came back and won the Del Mar Debutante by four lengths.

At about the same time the Debutante was going off, the Walters had this other horse named Cavonnier running in a small stakes at Bay Meadows. He had just broken his maiden at Santa Rosa, and somebody had told me he was a pretty nice horse. Just before post time for the Debutante, I went back and watched the race at Bay Meadows. Cavonnier came from off the pace and won, going five and a half furlongs in a quick 1:03⅗. I went back to the box and told Mr. Walter, "Hey, I need that horse down here." After Batroyale won, Mr. Walter said he'd ship him down the next day.

I waited for him, but he didn't show up. I was wondering where the hell he was, then I found out they had shipped him by mistake to Derek Meredith, who was training for them at the time, but wasn't having any luck. Poor old Derek saw this horse and thought, "Man, what a good-looking horse." He thought maybe the Walters had thrown him another bone, but I went to his barn and had to tell him the horse was supposed to go to me. Derek told me, "I didn't want to say anything when I saw him, because I thought it was too good to be true."

I ran Cavonnier back in the Del Mar Futurity and he finished third at 19-1. After a rough trip in the Norfolk Stakes, in which he finished fifth, I put him back with Cal-breds and he won the California Stallion Stakes and Cal Cup Juvenile. But then he got beat a head in the California Breeders' Champion Stakes at 4-5 and I was upset, because he shouldn't have lost that race.

I started getting Derby fever a little when he won the El Camino Real Derby at Bay Meadows in his three-year-old debut. Then he was fifth in the San Rafael and third in the San Felipe, but he ran well in the San Felipe, taking the lead very early and holding tough in the stretch. That wasn't his style of running at all. So I ran him back in the Santa Anita Derby and he went off at 10-1.

I couldn't believe it when he burst through horses and won comfortably. I was so excited and screamed so loudly, my stomach started to hurt. When I went down to the winner's circle, my stomach was killing me from these cramps. Poor Mrs. Walter was so sick, she couldn't come for the race and had to watch it on TV. That same day, my son Taylor had a baseball game, and Sherry asked me if she should come out or go to the baseball game. I told her, "I don't know. If I'm lucky, I'll run third." In fact, I almost ran him in an easier spot, but he was training so well, I told the Walters I wanted to give him one more shot against these horses, and they were fine with it.

One thing about winning the Santa Anita Derby, not only are you winning the Santa Anita Derby, but you know you're heading to the Kentucky Derby. I was so pumped up when I ran down there. They told me they wanted to interview me on ABC. I remember telling Al Michaels, "You have no idea how long I've wanted to be up on this stand talking to you." Then I looked down at the monitor and saw myself, and I couldn't help it. I smiled and gave myself a big thumbs up. I was like a little kid. Everyone got a big kick out of that. I think they knew right then that it was going to be a fun time in Louisville. I called the Executive West and said, "Hey, I'm comin' to town."

Like I said, in this business, don't ever burn your bridges.

CHAPTER 13

THE FISH

"I want to thank Mike Pegram. Without him, I would have never been here. You got me from the Quarter Horses and told me to come try Thoroughbreds. So, Mike, this is for you, my man."

— *Bob Baffert on national TV following*
Silver Charm's Kentucky Derby victory

In 1995, Bob Roth got out of the Thoroughbreds. He was having health problems and just wasn't having fun anymore. He died a couple of years later. It's just too bad he wasn't part of the whole Real Quiet scene. He was a real fun guy and he would have loved it. He and Mike made a great team.

Mike and I began going to the different sales, and he'd usually spend about five hundred thousand. We never had much luck buying expensive horses, so we didn't like spending over a hundred thousand for a horse. We'd go for numbers and try to pick up little freaks. That's where we had most of our success. For example, I paid thirty-seven thousand for High Stakes Player and he's earned over $800,000.

I was at the 1996 Keeneland September yearling sale, and I was sitting on the wall out by the walking ring. Mike was still on his way and hadn't arrived in Kentucky yet. The McKathan brothers, J. B. and Kevin, were with me. They had begun breaking my horses after my regular guy Jimmy Gladwell went private. As I was sitting there,

144

I saw this one horse from far away and he looked good. I was too lazy to get off the wall, so I told J. B. to go over and check the colt out and give me the word. He jumped off the wall and went over to look at him. After looking him over for a while, J. B. came back and said, "He doesn't look too bad, but he's a little crooked in the front legs." I got off the wall and went to look at him myself.

I liked him anyway, and I told J. B. I was willing to go to $50,000 or $60,000 for him. We followed him up to the pavilion, and the bidding was creeping along at around $12-$13,000. I couldn't believe it. I asked if there were any announcements made on this horse that I might have missed. There weren't any, so I wound up buying him for $17,000. I said to J. B., "Man, $17, 000. I can't believe I got him for so cheap." I started thinking, "I should just buy this horse for myself."

But I decided not to, because if he turned out to be a runner, I would have to give him to Mike anyway. So, I just put Mike's name on the slip. Mike finally showed up, and that night we met at Dudley's for dinner. He asked me, "So what did we get?" I told him we got one, a Quiet American colt. He looked him up in the catalogue and asked how much he went for, and I told him seventeen thousand. He says, "What does he have, cancer?"

I tell him, "No, he's kind of aerodynamic. He looks good from the side, but there isn't a lot to him from the front, and he's a little crooked." Mike rolls his eyes and goes, "Oh boy." Then, J. B. picks up a menu and holds up the cover to Mike. He says, "Mike, let me tell you something. I'll tell you what he looks like. You know, when you look in a fish tank and you see a fish that's so beautiful from the side? Then, he turns and swims toward you and there's nothing there?" While he's saying that, he turns the menu to the side to illustrate it to Mike. "Well, that's what this colt is like," he says.

After that, we started calling him "The Fish." We would have named him The Fish, but he had already been named Real Quiet, and Mike is very superstitious about changing a horse's name. Every time we had done that, the horse either got hurt or just didn't work out. What we did, though, is put "The Fish" on his halter.

After Real Quiet turned two, I sent him to Churchill Downs with Silver Charm. I had one other two-year-old colt with him, a big, good-looking dude named Johnbill. Right before Silver Charm won the Derby, some people from *The Blood-Horse* magazine came by and said they were doing a video on conformation, and asked if I could pick one of my horses and discuss his conformation, pointing out the strengths and flaws. It was late in the day, and the only horses who weren't done up with bandages were High Stakes Player and Real Quiet. So I brought Real Quiet out. I said on the video that he had a nice neck and shoulder and was well-balanced. But in the front, he was a little narrow and toed-out. I explained that I could live with that, because he wasn't going to be that quick and fast and would hold up under pressure.

We were really high on the horse, because he had worked so well at Churchill. But we just couldn't get him to break his maiden. He ran badly first time out at Churchill, then finished third. Afterward, I got a call from this bloodstock agent who offered two hundred thousand for him. I still thought he'd be a nice horse down the road, so I told him we weren't interested. If I had owned him, he would have been gone.

I sent him to California and he was third again at Hollywood. He was a real timid horse with a big, long stride. If you worked him from the pole, he'd work good, but out of the gate, he was really slow. It took him a long time to get going. He wasn't nominated to the Breeders' Cup, so I nominated him to the Indian Nations

Futurity at Santa Fe, New Mexico. It was a $500,000 purse, and I decided to send him there for the trial. He showed good speed on the rail, but tired to finish third. I ran him back in the Futurity, and they just got away from him. He was on the inside, eating a lot of dirt, and he couldn't stand getting hit in the face with dirt. He closed ground and finished third again.

After I got him back home, I was mad at the horse for losing two races at Santa Fe, so I ran him back just two weeks later, even though he had just shipped back from New Mexico on a van. He ran at Del Mar and was fourth, beaten eight lengths. That was a bad race. Scott Stevens, Gary's brother, was on him, and he said every time the dirt hit him, he shied away from it. He just wouldn't run into it at all. He said, "Man, he needs blinkers really bad."

I put blinkers on him and he worked really well with them. I stretched him out to a mile and a sixteenth, and he broke his maiden by three lengths at Santa Anita. I sent him to Churchill for the Kentucky Jockey Club Stakes and he trained awesome. Kent Desormeaux, who was on him when he broke his maiden, couldn't ride him, so I put David Flores on. He broke a little slow and he had to check three times, but he was flying at the end, finishing third. He should have won that race. I sent him back home and nine days later he worked five furlongs in :58 and change. That race obviously had taken nothing out of him, so I told Mike I wanted to run him right back. I put him in the Hollywood Futurity and he won in very fast time. He really looked good, and we started thinking we had something here.

I gave him some time off and freshened him. Meanwhile, on New Year's Day, I ran one of Mike's fillies, Fun in Excess, in a little stakes and she won it as the third or fourth choice. It was one of those $75,000 overnight stakes, and I didn't even know the name

147

of it. I was in the winner's circle, and I looked down at the program and saw that the name of the race was the Run for the Roses. I said, "I'll be a sonofagun." I told Mike right then and there, "You know what? You're gonna win the Kentucky Derby this year with Real Quiet." I told him, "Think back. First, *The Blood-Horse* comes by to do this video, and of all my horses, I just happen to choose him to bring out. Then, I dedicate my Derby win to you on national TV. Then we win the Hollywood Futurity, and now, the first stakes of the year, we win the Run for the Roses. I'm telling you, the planets are lining up here."

After Real Quiet turned three, I needed to find a two-turn race for him, and the only one was the Golden Gate Derby on January 18. I took P. A. with me and invited Ed Musselman, who put out a newsletter/tout sheet called "Indian Charlie." I had a three-year-old colt for Hal Earnhardt that we named Indian Charlie. He was a Cal-bred, but he looked like he could be something special. He had won his only start at two very impressively, but we had to take a chip out of his ankle. He was recovering nicely and was about a month away from a race.

We flew to San Francisco on Southwest Airlines, and the rain was really coming down as we were coming in to Oakland. We were bouncing around pretty good. It was pouring out, and you could barely see the airport. We came in for a landing, and the minute the plane touched down, it took off again. It hit once, then went straight back up. We started thinking, "This ain't right." The pilot didn't say a word, and we're all looking at each other like, "This is it. We're gonna hit a tower or something. We're all going to die."

We climbed straight up. I said I wished the pilot would come on and say something, and Injun Chuck says, "No way. I want to make sure he's got both hands on that steering wheel." Finally, after ten minutes, he came on and apologized, and said that they had some cross winds and didn't want to take any chances. And I'm thinking, "Hell, I think he just overshot the damn runway."

We finally landed, and things didn't get any better after that. I told Mike I should scratch Real Quiet, but I needed to get a race into him. When we got to the track, it was like a damn lake. Everyone told me I had to put jar caulks on the horse or I'd have no chance. They help a horse grab hold of the track better. But I wasn't about to put jar caulks on him, because he's crooked and I didn't want to take a chance of crippling him. Those jar caulks can hurt a horse more than help it. As it turned out, never at any time was he in the race. He was done turning for home and Kent just wrapped up on him. He finished dead-last and was beaten over twenty lengths. As soon as I got down there, the press got on me, asking me why I didn't have caulks on him. I told them this race wasn't that important to me and I wasn't about to take the chance of hurting him.

Going back to the airport, I told Mike, "You know, I'm such an idiot." I had just received my Eclipse Award as the top trainer of 1997, and I said, "They should take my Eclipse Award away for running this horse. I should have scratched him." Mike said he would have been all right with it. But there was no harm done, and we just decided to throw it out and go on from there.

When we got home, we scoped him and discovered he had a little ulcer in his throat, probably from all the mud. After that, I just freshened him up and got him going again. But he could have really gotten hurt in that race. In fact, a number of horses in the field did get hurt with the caulks on, and you didn't hear from them for a while.

I had two other good three-year-olds in the barn. Indian Charlie made his return a month later and won a Cal-bred allowance race by nine lengths in 1:21⅗. Souvenir Copy, one of the most talented horses I've ever had, had won the Del Mar Futurity and Norfolk Stakes at two, but he was displacing his palate, and we were having trouble with his breathing. Indian Charlie, however, was doing things in the morning that were unbelievable.

I ran Indian Charlie and Real Quiet on the same weekend. Indian Charlie was in against open company, and he overcame a lot for an inexperienced horse, winning a mile allowance race by two and a half lengths in 1:35. The next day, Real Quiet ran a huge race in the San Felipe, getting beat a head by Artax. One more jump and he would have won it. I ran both horses in the Santa Anita Derby, and the track was wet and fast, and they had sealed it. It wasn't Real Quiet's kind of track. I hadn't really trained him hard for the race, and although Kent dropped his rein and broke his whip, the horse still finished second, about two lengths behind Indian Charlie. Then we found out Real Quiet had bled a little in the race. He made the vet's list for bleeding, and nobody ever picked up on it.

I told Mike, he's definitely a Derby horse. We were in the show. That other horse just ran unbelievable. But even though Indian Charlie still was lightly raced, the Santa Anita Derby took a lot out of him. He would put out so much, then would quit eating for a couple of days after a race.

When we got to Kentucky, both horses trained great, but two weeks out, Real Quiet really started to come around. His last work before the Derby was unbelievable. I told Mike afterward, "Man, you're looking good. You've got a shot to win this thing." Indian Charlie still was working well, but he wasn't liking the track the way Real Quiet was.

On Derby Day, I told Gary Stevens that Indian Charlie was doing good, but he wasn't doing super. I told him I thought the only horse he had to worry about running by him in the stretch was Real

Quiet. I watched most of the other horses work, and the one I thought was training really well was the Arkansas Derby winner, Victory Gallop.

What was great about the 1998 Derby was that my mom and dad were there, and John Bassett was there. And also having horses in the race for Mike and Hal, who had been with me for so long. It was just unfortunate that there was a little rift in their friendship and they weren't as close as they had been.

I really enjoyed myself at the 1998 Derby, because I had already won with Silver Charm and I was here with two guys who were good friends of mine who were here to have a good time. Hal had sold part-interest in Indian Charlie to John Gaines, and all those people were great as well. So there was no real pressure. It was just fun.

Bassett really cracked me up after the race. He had been invited as Hal's guest. After Real Quiet wins and Indian Charlie runs third, I go down to the winner's circle, and I see this guy wearing a black cowboy hat crossing the track, and it's Bassett. I say to him, "Hey John, what did you do with Hal? Did you just leave him up there?" He goes, "Hell, I switched camps at the eighth pole. I'm with you guys now."

When I won the Derby with Silver Charm, it was for me. I had to win it. This one was mainly for my friends and my owners. I remember, as they neared the quarter pole, Indian Charlie was on the lead, but I could see that Gary was having to ride him a little bit. I'm saying to myself, "Oh man, he's starting to weaken." Then I see this horse on the outside making this big move, and before I could tell who it is, I'm thinking, "Well, I'm dead." All of a sudden, I see Mike's colors, and I yell out, "It's the Fish!" I'll never forget that.

When Real Quiet came down the stretch, my dad was all excited, and I thought for sure we were going to run one-two. Then Victory Gallop came charging on the outside, but in the last fifty yards I knew we had it, and all at once it hit me: "I can't believe I'm going to win the Kentucky Derby for Mike Pegram." I started thinking, Thank God, I'm getting this out of the way now, because the chances of me buying a Derby winner for seventeen grand again are pretty slim. I always asked how I could repay Mike for getting me started in the Thoroughbreds. And when they hit the wire, it was like, "Yes! We're even." We had come a long way since having a one-horse claiming stable.

After the Derby, Real Quiet worked great, but I didn't like the way Indian Charlie had worked. The girl on him came back and said he just didn't feel right. There just was no oomph to his stride. I called Hal and told him I didn't like the way he came out of the race and that I was going to pass the Preakness. As it turned out, he pulled a suspensory during a workout at Del Mar in late July and never ran again.

When you run in the Derby, you don't say, "I'm going to win this thing." You just say, "I've got a good shot to win it." But for the Preakness, I knew I was going to win. He trained so unbelievable, and when he drew post eleven, it just made me sick. But I still felt he couldn't lose. He ran a fantastic race, winning easily despite going wide on both turns, something you don't do at Pimlico with those sharp turns.

He looked good when I got him back to Churchill, but he picked up a little fever. What had happened was that he was completely dehydrated. It was so hot at the Preakness, and then I flew him right back. I gave him five or six days off of just walking, and gave him plenty of fluids every day. Then he started eating again, and I could tell he was back.

Like in the Preakness, I thought he couldn't lose the Belmont. But Kent got a little excited there and he might have made an early move, but I really don't put any blame on him. That's a lot of pressure to put on a jockey. Real Quiet looked like he was home free at the three-sixteenths pole, but then Victory Gallop came charging out of the pack, and they hit the wire together. When they put up Victory Gallop's number, it was really disappointing. Not so much narrowly losing the Triple Crown again, but because I felt like I got cheated. He had it, and it all came apart at the end. Victory Gallop was in front only for that one jump. Real Quiet had his head in front one jump before the wire and one jump after the wire, and never gave it up after that.

I was standing there holding my daughter Savannah when they posted the result. I said to Sherry how terrible it was to come this far and get beat like that. And Sherry kept saying, "I'm so sorry." She knew all the time I had put in to get here. Just then, Savannah grabbed my cheeks and said, "But Daddy, you still have me." And that was a killer. I told her, "Yes, honey, I still have you. That's all that matters." That brought me right out of it.

The one thing about the Belmont that was wonderful was the fact that over 80,000 people showed up for the race. It was so great for the sport and I was just glad to contribute to it.

I took Real Quiet back to California, and I was going to get him ready for the Haskell at Monmouth. But when I worked him at Del Mar, he just wasn't as aggressive as usual. He wasn't picking up the bit and was just going through the motions. It didn't feel right. He had lost some weight, so I told Mike I wanted to ease up on him. He just wasn't enjoying what he was doing. He said fine, so we gave him the rest of the year off.

Once again, like the previous year, no one was able to step up and claim the three-year-old championship, so we got our second straight Eclipse Award.

That spring was exciting not only because of Real Quiet and Indian Charlie, but we also went to the Dubai World Cup with Silver Charm. Earlier, we had been gearing up for the big showdown with Gentlemen in the Santa Anita Handicap. Things had begun to really build up and Santa Anita had spent a lot of money to promote the race. Then, a few days before the race, we noticed Silver Charm was a little off in front, and he'd never limped before in his life. He had been shod, and we figured it had to be his shoes, so we took the heel nails out of the one shoe. He seemed fine after that, and we entered him in the race. But the next day, he was off in the other foot, so we took the heel nails off that one as well, but he still was off and you could tell it was bugging him. He stood off in the corner of his stall and he had his ears pinned.

I called up Bob Lewis and told him we were going to run some tests to find out what was wrong. I had another veterinarian come in to look at him and he said it was the nails, and that we should just soak it. I was really devastated. But I found out from Gentlemen's trainer Dick Mandella months later that if I had run, he would have scratched his horse. Gentlemen wasn't doing well either. He had this bad skin rash, but when I scratched, Dick looked at the field and decided Gentlemen could still just gallop around there and beat those horses. As it turned out, he was 1-20 in the Big 'Cap and finished last in a four-horse field.

After we scratched, there were many people who believed there really was nothing wrong with him. It's funny, I remember many times I would run one of my horses and he was doing well, and I'd hear rumors he was sore. Finally, I have a horse who was lame and nobody believed me. It's like I wanted to shout, "I'm telling you, he's lame."

About three days later, he was doing well and looked good out on the track, so I called Bob Lewis and told him we could either go to the Oaklawn Handicap or go to Dubai. I said I'd like to go to Dubai if it was okay with him, and he told me anywhere I wanted to go was fine.

Dubai was a great experience. I sent Eoin there with Silver Charm and he called and told me the horse traveled great. When I got off the plane, everything was totally different than I had imagined. The first person I saw was a soldier standing on the runway with an Uzi machine gun. I said to him, "Hey, you must be a bad shot if you got an Uzi." He didn't think that was very funny.

I was expecting Dubai to look like something out of the Gulf War, with deserted cars along the road, but everything was very beautiful and clean, and I was really impressed. Silver Charm was in this big, white air-conditioned stall. For a horse, it was like staying at the Ritz. Bill and P. A. showed up, and we hit all the parties. Sheikh Mohammed, who owns the racetrack and rules the country with his brothers Hamdan and Maktoum, really knows how to put on a show.

When I took Silver Charm over for the race, he had his head down and his bottom lip was hanging, and it looked like he was falling asleep. I said, "What the hell is going on here? We're losing him." I put ice water over his head to try to revive him. I really didn't know what to expect.

When I got him to the paddock, I told Gary Stevens, "He's a little quiet. You may have to wake him up a little bit." Gary said, "That's okay. We want him quiet." When I watched him go off with the pony, I could see he was getting into the bit, so I felt a lot better. By the time he got to the gate, he was really sharp.

Early in the race, he was laying right off the pace, and all I was thinking was I hope he shows up and doesn't embarrass me. When they hit the half-mile pole, he was moving good, and by the time they turned for home and headed down that long stretch, I was convinced he was just going to open up on the field. Then, they came to him from both sides, and I turned to Bill and said, "Oh man, he's gonna run third. They're going by him." Then, just like that, he kicked back in again, and that was an awesome thing to watch. He opened up again, but suddenly here came Swain charging at him from the outside. He dug in and held on to win by a nose.

I thought he had won, but I wasn't sure. Just then, I looked down and saw Sheikh Mohammed looking back at us. His Godolphin Stable was the owner of Swain. He looked up at me and gave me a thumbs up. I said to Bill, "Hey, Sheikh Mo just gave me the thumbs up. I don't know if there's a photo, but that's good enough for me. This is his deal, so I think we're okay." When I saw the photo and realized he had won by just a couple of inches, I started wondering if the thumbs up was for me or the photo guy.

It was amazing. The Sheikh had just lost by a nose and he was real excited for us. He was there with his son and his brothers, and he wanted to touch the horse. Between the race, the hotel, the party in the desert, and everything else, it was a fantastic experience. It's a long trip back, especially if you don't win, and let me tell you, we partied all the way home. To me, it was a great training feat to win this race and to see the Charm put on a show like that. I was just proud to be a part of it.

SAYING GOODBYE

"Bobby has always been a horseman before anything. First he was a horseman, then he became a trainer, and then he became a media celebrity. He has our dad to thank for putting him through all the hoops. Bobby has been blessed when it comes to the horses. He's achieved everything he set out to do, but you know the expression, 'Be careful what you wish for, because it may come true.' Bobby has always been an eternal optimist and very positive about everything, and because of that, sometimes he doesn't see the future clearly. He always thinks everything is going to turn out okay. You have to give him credit for taking his career, which is just a horse trainer no matter how you look at it, and raising it to a new level. Bobby has done a helluva job promoting not only the sport but himself. It's amazing how similar both he and Lukas are. Both taught, both came up with the Quarter Horses, both are great self promoters, and here they are at the top of the Thoroughbred world."
— *Bill Baffert*

Silver Charm has had his critics, but I think the Dubai World Cup stamped him as more than just another horse who won a Triple Crown race. When he got back from Dubai, I laid him off for a while and he got real heavy on me. I brought him to Kentucky and basically just showed him off, like the big pet that he was.

I decided I wanted to do something for Bob Lewis, so a week after Real Quiet's Derby, I had Tony Leonard, one of the top equine photographers, come out to the track. I decked Silver Charm out in

Arab garb that was given to me in Dubai, and dressed up in my dish-dasha, the familiar white Arabian garment which I also got in Dubai. Then, I brought the horse out by the gap to the track, with the Twin Spires in the background, and got up on his back. He wasn't too thrilled with the situation, but Tony did manage to get a good shot, which appeared in *The Blood-Horse* and *Daily Racing Form*. I made up a nice print and gave it to the Lewises.

I started back training the horse, and Churchill Downs told me they were bumping the purse of the Stephen Foster to $750,000 and asked if I thought I could have him ready to run by then. I only had thirty days to get him ready, so I put a super rush job on him. Then, the weights came out and it was ridiculous. They weighted him at 127, with Awesome Again at 113. I would have backed out, but I had already told them I'd run the horse. And I was already starting to get criticized a little in the press for ducking Skip Away.

People think the so-called feud I had with Skip Away's trainer Sonny Hine started around this time. But any friction between us actually began in Texas the year before. Sonny showed up for the Texas Mile with Skip Away and I came with Isitingood and Semoran. When I saw Sonny down there, he asked me, "Why did you come here? I was doing them a favor. Why did you have to bring your horses?" Well, they had raised the pot to three hundred and fifty grand, and I came for the money. The race was too short for Skippy and he didn't fire that day.

Semoran had drawn the seven post and Skippy was in the eight. On paper, it looked like Skippy was going to blow us away. So, before the race, I told Semoran's owner Don Dizney, "You know, our only chance is to float ol' Skippy out on that first turn. I just want to know if it's okay with you if we do that?" I asked him, because I had two different owners. Mike Pegram was the principal owner of Isitingood.

Don said it was fine, so I told Russell Baze, who was on Semoran, "You might want to float Skip Away out a little bit on that first turn." And Baze said, "Hell, I can put him out there with the ponies if you want." I told him, "Yeah, do what you have to."

Isitingood broke like a shot from the rail, and Skip Away broke a little slow. Semoran got caught a bit wide himself, but Baze kept him super wide, and Skippy wound up going about seven or eight wide on the first turn. Isitingood went on to win the race and Skip Away finished third without threatening at all. I think that was the first bit of resentment on Sonny's part. But when he sent Skippy out to Hollywood for the Breeders' Cup Classic later that year, we got along pretty well. In fact, after Skippy won the race easily, I said nothing but great things about the horse. I thought he ran a sensational race and should have been Horse of the Year.

The problems really started after I got back from Dubai, and the experts ranked Silver Charm over Skip Away in the weekly poll. Sonny claimed Silver Charm had beaten nothing but a bunch of turf horses in Dubai and asked why he didn't come looking for Skip Away to settle who was the best horse. When Skip Away won the Pimlico Special for his fifth straight stakes win, Sonny was at it again, saying we were ducking him by staying in Kentucky and waiting for the Stephen Foster.

Three weeks later, Skip Away won the Massachusetts Handicap, and that's when things really came to a boil. After the race, a reporter called and told me Sonny had called me a coward. I told him there was no way Sonny would say that. In this game you can knock another trainer to your friends, but you never do it in the press. So the reporter played me his tape of Sonny after the MassCap, and he pretty much did call me a coward, saying, "A coward never wins." So I said, "That doesn't sound like Sonny Hine, that sounds like

Elmer Fudd." Well, then that got out and the media had a field day with it. They quoted Sonny calling me a coward and me calling Sonny Elmer Fudd.

I only said that because Sonny has this whine in his voice like Elmer Fudd. In fact, some people called him Sonny Whine. But Sonny's wife, Carolyn, took it badly, because Sonny was suffering from this disease called Bell's Palsy that affected his facial muscles, and she thought I was making fun of that. But I didn't know anything about it. If I had known he was ill I never would have said that. After they told me, I felt really bad about it.

The truth is, I thought Sonny did a helluva job with that horse. Unfortunately, the media kept this feud alive all the way through the Breeders' Cup. Actually, it could have been a fun deal, but Sonny and Carolyn took it to a personal level. I tried to back off, but Sonny kept knocking Silver Charm. I never knocked Skip Away, but he would always knock Silver Charm. Even Bob Lewis was getting a little agitated, saying, "We've got to go beat that horse." I told Bob, "Don't worry about it. Skip Away is a good horse, but we'll have our turn. When we're ready, we'll run against him. But we're not ready yet."

After Silver Charm finished second in the Stephen Foster, I was going to hook Skippy in the Hollywood Gold Cup, but my horse got sick on me from the shipping and it knocked him out a little. Skip Away went on to win the Hollywood Gold Cup for his seventh straight, and combined with Silver Charm's loss, it put him on top in the polls.

I had to put Silver Charm on heavy-duty antibiotics, because a number of my two-year-olds had gotten pretty sick, and one of them died. I lost a lot of training with him, and he got real fat and heavy on me again. I thought I'd run him at a mile and a sixteenth in the San Diego Handicap at Del Mar to set him up for the Pacific Classic.

But it was real hot and humid the day of the race, and when I saw him in the paddock, I could tell he was just too heavy. He was ready to run five-eighths of a mile and that's what he did. He got real tired, and Gary didn't push him after that. He wound up fifth and last, beaten a city block. It was the first time in his career he had turned in a bad performance.

After the race, Bob Lewis looked over at me, and I told him, "Don't worry, he's okay." I knew deep down I ran a super short horse. Gary told me he had no horse down the backside. He felt he wasn't going anywhere, and because the horse is so gutsy, Gary knew he'd keep on trying to hook those horses even though he was tired, so he wrapped up on him. That made it look worse than it really was.

When I started training Silver Charm again, I had Chris McCarron work him three-quarters out of the gate. I have a lot of respect for Chris and I said to him, "You work him, then tell me if you think he's washed up." He walked in the gate with his head down and he was completely relaxed. I thought for sure he wasn't going to work at all, but the late Willard Proctor was working some maiden from the gate at the same time. And when the gate opened, Silver Charm just burst out of there and beat the other horse by some twenty lengths. They caught him in 1:11 and change. When he came back, I went, "Chris, do I need to retire him?" And Chris says, "Do I get to ride him?" I tell him no, and he says, "Retire him."

Chris loved the way he worked, so I kept on jammin' on him and jammin' on him. I sent him to Turfway Park for the Kentucky Cup Classic, and I told Bob Lewis, "This is the make-or-break race. He's gonna have to run good." He wound up running a helluva race, coming back again to dead-heat for the win with Wild Rush, who had won the Metropolitan Handicap earlier that year. The time of 1:47⅗ was incredible on a dead track. I thought for sure he was beaten at the eighth pole, but he fought back like the old Silver Charm. It was a great win and showed everyone he was back. Then he went back to California and beat Free House in the Goodwood Handicap, and that set him up for his long-awaited showdown with Skip Away in the Breeders' Cup Classic. Skippy had won two more stakes after the Hollywood Gold Cup before finishing third in the slop in the Jockey Club Gold Cup.

That loss, combined with the Charm's two stakes victories, put us back in the running for Horse of the Year. But I felt he started tailing off on me a little bit coming up to the Breeders' Cup. He was training good, but not awesome. He ran a good race and tried hard, but Awesome Again came through between horses to beat him three-quarters of a length, with Skip Away finishing sixth.

In 1999, Silver Charm ran two good thirds, in the Donn and Santa Anita Handicaps, and I felt he should have won the Big 'Cap. Gary gave him a lot to do, and he was flying at the end, beaten a length by his old rival Free House. We sent him to Dubai again, and although a lot of people criticized me for going over there again, I really thought he couldn't lose that race. He trained good, but on the night of the race, he didn't seem quite as sharp as he had the previous year. He bled during the race and ran badly. When he came home and finished a dull fourth in the Stephen Foster in June of '99, Bob Lewis and I decided it was time to retire him.

I became so attached to this horse. He was like my fifth child. I wanted that Kentucky Derby win so badly and he gave it to me. For three years, he was always there for me, and every day I would look forward to getting to the barn and seeing him. I got so used to seeing that gray head peering over the webbing, looking for his carrots. And I could always hear him nickering from my office. When he left, I felt like I had lost a good friend.

I had reached the top of my profession, but sometimes success comes at a cost. In order to compete at the championship level, you have to be married to these horses and be on the road constantly. And sometimes that can put a strain on your real marriage. Sherry is a wonderful woman and a fantastic mother, and has done a super job raising our kids. But motherhood made it difficult for her to get involved like I would have wanted her to. It was like we've lived two separate lives.

At the track, however, everything was going great. We had one top horse after another and I was really on a roll. In addition to all my top colts, we had Silverbulletday for Mike Pegram and the home-bred Excellent Meeting for Mr. and Mrs. John Mabee, and they proceeded to sweep just about every major two-year-old and three-year-old filly race in the country. To have them run one-two in the Breeders' Cup Juvenile Fillies was exciting, but I really got a super thrill winning the Kentucky Oaks with Silverbulletday. Here, Mike Pegram wins the Kentucky Derby one year, then comes back and wins the Kentucky Oaks the next year. It was unbelievable.

I remember the day we bought Silverbulletday. The Keeneland July yearling sale was over, and the McKathan brothers and I stayed around for the Fasig-Tipton yearling sale. That is the hottest sale in the country, literally. For some reason, the air is always stagnant; there's never a breeze. If you can take the heat, you can find a runner there, but because of the heat, you get tired of looking at horses very quickly. I had just bought a yearling at Keeneland, later to be named Forestry, for a sale-high $1,500,000, and we were really pumped. I had bought him for a new client, Aaron Jones, a lumber tycoon who had been in the game for many years.

Then, at the Fasig-Tipton sale, I bought the highest-priced yearling there for $290,000 for Bob Lewis, and that was Straight Man.

There was nothing else at the sale that we liked, and it was getting really hot and miserable, so I started thinking about leaving. I hate to leave sales, so I asked J. B. if there was anything we had missed. J. B. told me that was it; that was all they had. J. B. and Kevin weed out the bad ones. This way I don't have to spend all my time looking at all these horses. It's worth it for me to pay them five percent of every purchase price to go there early and do all the work.

They then make a list of about ten or fifteen they like and I go look at them. By the time I get there, they've done two days of sweating and looking and listening. They know what's going on. I'll come and I might like one or two, but I'll nix most of them. I'll also look at some of the ones I picked out earlier on pedigree. I'll vet the ones I like and then wait. That's all there is to it. They do all the hard work. On many occasions, when consignors know who the big buyers are, they'll come over and tell us who their best horses are and which are ones we should look at.

We were just getting ready to leave the Fasig-Tipton sale when I saw this filly walking into the back of the ring, and she was beautiful. I asked J. B. if he had looked at her, and he said they had, but she wasn't on the list. I took a close look at her and noticed that her knees were a little bit offset. J. B. figured he must have looked at her in the stall and saw the offset knees, so he just walked off. In that heat, you just can't concentrate on every horse.

I watched her walk around the ring and told J. B., "Man, she is beautiful. I'm buying this one." I waited and bid from way outside the ring underneath a tree. I told Kevin to get the guy's attention, because I didn't want anyone to see me bidding on this filly. I was going to try to steal her. I thought I could get her for about fifty or sixty thousand. I made my bids from out back, and she goes to eighty, ninety, a hundred thousand. I couldn't believe it. Soon, she's up to

$150,000, and I'm going, "Sonofabitch." I finally bid $155,000 and it stopped right there.

I never did find out who the underbidder was, but after she broke her maiden by eleven lengths, there were about ten underbidders who came out of the woodwork. The only horse I ever bought in which no underbidder ever came forward was Real Quiet. I figured it was some guy from Wyoming or someplace who doesn't even know he was the underbidder. I didn't even find out until after the Derby that the guy who had sold him had had his legs wired to make them look straighter. When he finally told me, I felt like I had bought Forrest Gump.

During the Fasig-Tipton sale, Mike had called me just to check in and see what was going on, and I told him there really was nothing I liked. Then, after I bought the filly, I called him back and said I just found this filly I loved and told him what I had paid for her. I said, "She's a beautiful sonofagun. I know you don't like to spend more than a hundred grand, but I don't think I'll be able to find you a horse I like for that price." I also told him if this filly had been in the July sale she would have brought a half a million. I said she was a little off-set and the dam hadn't had a runner, but she looked awesome. I told him if he didn't want her it was no big deal, I'd find someone else.

In the meantime, I had signed the ticket Morning Wood Stables, which is nobody. It's just a name. I use it whenever I don't know who I'm buying a horse for. I didn't know how she was going to vet, so I wasn't about to sign her over to somebody before I found out.

One thing about Mike, he knows when I really love a horse. He said if I liked her, he'd take her. He told me to have them change it to his name, but I said I'd keep it as Morning Wood Stables, and when he got the bill for her to just pay it.

J. B. and Kevin took her down to Florida to break her, and they really loved her right from the start. When they sent her to me, she was ready. When I first got her, she was ready to work, and the first time I breezed her, I knew we had something special.

I actually was more excited about the Oaks this year than I was about the Derby. I know I had a chance to become the first trainer ever to win three consecutive Kentucky Derbys, but I had never won the Oaks, and we had been looking forward to the race since the day Silverbulletday broke her maiden at Churchill on the day of the '98 Stephen Foster. And I really didn't think that much about the Derby because I was convinced I was going to win it anyway. I think I had gotten a little spoiled.

Then, when I heard they were going to have twenty horses in the race, it was hard for me to get into it. I knew General Challenge was the most talented and gifted horse in the field — probably the most talented and gifted horse I ever trained — but he just didn't have the mind to cope with a field that large. He lacked a lot upstairs. And Prime Timber and Excellent Meeting were both come-from-behind horses and I realized they were going to need a lot of luck. So, it's hard to get that excited when you know you're going to need more luck than horse. And of course, we didn't get the luck. General Challenge got banged around pretty good and came back a mess.

I'll never forget the day Silverbulletday broke her maiden, Mike said to me, "Well, there's our Oaks winner." I told him, "Oaks, hell, that could be our Derby winner." I knew that day, if I was going to win the Oaks, this was the filly to do it.

I was really looking forward to running Silverbulletday in the Preakness, and it was so disappointing when we drew the outside. I was really bummed out over that. When we had to run her in the Black-Eyed Susan Stakes instead the day before, it was like kissing your sister. It was great that she won, but there was really no excitement at all. On Preakness Day, Mike and I walked up to the fence in the infield. Everyone remembered us from the previous year and were screaming for us to come over. It was a wild scene, which ended with Mike chugging a beer through the fence with a funnel.

What was exciting was going to the Belmont. It was the first Belmont I've really enjoyed. There was no pressure, not having to go for the Triple Crown. We were stabled way out by ourselves and didn't have to deal with the media. And most of all, it was great, because Mike and I and the McKathan brothers all stayed in New York City and we had a ball.

I knew what we were up against in the race, but I felt if Silverbulletday got to run the way she wanted, she had a big chance. But I told Jerry Bailey in the paddock, "If you're out there cookin' and they're on you all the way, don't push her if it looks like she's had it turning for home." I told him I thought she could get it with the right trip, but if there's any doubt at all turning for home, just wrap up on her. I said he could pull her up or ease her, I didn't care. I would take the rap for it. These top-class, talented horses still try so hard even when they're tired, and that's when they get hurt.

As it turned out, Charismatic wound up breathing down her throat the whole way, and Jerry wisely took a hold of her and didn't push her. She might have run fourth at best. After the race, I saw Bob Lewis, who had just watched Charismatic pull up past the wire and get hauled off in an ambulance. I tried to reassure him, telling him they'll probably be able to save the horse. After talking to Mike, I went upstairs with P. A. to where the Lewises had all their friends, and I stayed with them while Bob went back to the barn to check on the horse. I knew most of them from Silver Charm's Triple Crown.

Mike, meanwhile, had three limos that were to pick him and his friends up and take them back to the barn. But only two limos showed up, so Mike, J. B., and Kevin walked back. The New York Racing Association security guy who looked after me also walked back with them.

When I got back to the barn, I see the guys and they've got dirt all over them, and there are blood stains on their shirts. But it wasn't from them. I ask them what the hell happened, and they fill me in on all the details.

They're all walking back along this chain link fence outside the stable area that divides the incoming and outgoing traffic. Mike and his group are on one side of the fence and this other guy is on the other side, giving the security guy a lot of grief about the way he's dressed. He was with some friends of his and he kept mouthing off. Finally, Mike tells the guy, "You better shut your mouth. I just lost twenty thousand dollars and I don't need to be listening to your shit."

The other guy, who had too much to drink, keeps at it, saying to Mike, "Who the hell do you think you are?" And Mike tells him, "You better shut your mouth, because you're fixing to run out of fence up here." The guy and his friends keep following them along the fence until it ended. As soon as they get to the end, the guy goes up to Mike and says, "Okay, big boy, what are you going to do about it?" He goes to take a swing at Mike, and Mike just decks him. The next thing you know, Mike is on top of him, and five of the guy's friends jump Mike from behind.

Things are now starting to get pretty wild. Just then, one of the limos drives by and some of Mike's friends from his hometown of Princeton, Indiana, jump out and join in. This one Indiana guy starts fighting with someone, who grabs his tie and tries to jerk him down. But he doesn't realize that these guys are from Princeton, Indiana, and they don't really dress up over there. So when he goes to jerk on his tie, all he's got in his hand is the ugliest-looking maroon clip-on tie. While he's looking at this tie, trying to figure out what the hell happened, the guy from Princeton flattens him.

The guy Kevin was fighting was a true sportsman. Kevin hits him a couple of times, and his Rolex watch comes undone. He goes, "Hold it, I've got to fix my watch." So the guy stops, and Kevin snaps it back on and hits him again.

Finally, these guys must have thought they were dealing with professionals — especially when the tie came off — and they all got up and took off. They had had enough. Mike said he had a ball. He said he felt like he was back home in Princeton again. When Mike got back to the barn, the first thing he said was, "You know what? I feel much better. I got my twenty thousand dollars worth out of that deal. We may have lost the race at 5:30, but we won the fight at 5:45."

HIGH ROLLER

"Beverly and I have had an eight-year association with Bob, and I don't mean to shy away from anything that is controversial, but it's really been a delight from start to finish. I say that simply because, look where he's taken us. The first horse he ever bought for us became a stakes winner, and he's continued to come up with outstanding horses for us, among them, of course, Silver Charm. We're not only grateful, but we've come to know and love the Baffert family. I've often said this, and I meant it somewhat in humor, but if he were available, I think I'd have adopted him as a son. Of course, all sons deserve a spanking once in a while, and when I offered to bet him two hundred thousand dollars horse for horse — Charismatic against Silverbulletday in the Belmont Stakes — it was meant as a little trip to the woodshed. But Bob is one of those people in my viewpoint whose glass is always half full or more, and anyone who is enthusiastic about the industry can't help but be pleased to be associated with a winner such as Bob Baffert. He's lots of fun and keeps your spirits up when they might otherwise be down, and I like that, because I'm not one who deals well with spirits that are down."
— Bob Lewis

've always called the horses I buy at the sales "ham sandwiches." I made a career of winning major stakes with cheap horses I picked out. But those days are gone. Although I still like to find the ham sandwiches, I'm now playing in the major leagues. There's no way a few years ago I could have envisioned myself in a bidding war with guys like Lukas and Demi O'Byrne, who buys for the Coolmore group. But here I was at the 1997 Keeneland summer yearling sale, bidding on the sales topper for an owner I had never even met. When it was over, I could barely sign the sales slip, my hands were shaking so much.

Following Silver Charm's Triple Crown, Bob Lewis asked me if I was going to the Keeneland July sale, and I told him I was. He said to make sure I went, because he was looking to buy some horses. I was thinking I finally got my foot back in the door with him. When I ran into Bob at the sale I told him I had a few horses I was really interested in, and one filly in particular. He had Wayne with him, and he said to me, "Well, Bob, I just want you to know that that horse is already on Wayne's list." He showed me Wayne's list, and shit, there were about two hundred horses in the catalogue and he had a hundred of them down there.

My first reaction was, "Man, that stinks." I thought I was back in with Bob, but it was obvious Wayne was still in the old driver's seat. I was never one to ask Bob what the deal was with anything. He's such a nice guy, I didn't want to question him. I just said to myself, "What the hell. That's the way it is."

When I saw the McKathan brothers, I told them, "Well, I guess there's no use looking anymore. It seems like we're on the outside looking in again." I have to admit I was sort of pissed off, so I told them I might as well catch the first plane out of there. I said, "It's just hard for me to compete with Wayne for older clients. He's got a gift; he seems to put them under hypnosis."

Just then, Frank Taylor of Taylor Made Farm came up to me and asked me what my mobile phone number was. He said someone has been trying to get a hold of me, and told me that I'd be getting a call. He said that was all he could tell me. I'm wondering what the hell he was talking about. A half an hour later my phone rings, and I hear, "Hello, Bob, this is Aaron. Aaron Jones. I don't know if you know me." I told him, "I don't know you, but I know of you."

He said he hadn't been having a lot of luck in racing recently. He had spent $7 million buying horses and had earned only about $120,000 of it back. He told me he had been watching the Triple Crown races with his wife, Marie, and they saw how much fun Bob Lewis was having. He and Bob had gone to the same school together. Marie told him, "How come we're not having fun like that?"

He told me, "I've hired every damn agent I can find to buy me horses, and I'm just not having any luck. I just want to know, do you see anything you like there?" Then he asked me who I was buying for, and I told him I came to buy for Bob Lewis, but I sort of got shuffled back in the pack, because Lukas is buying all his horses.

He said, "Well, I've never done anything like this before. Usually, I like to be there, but I trust you and I've heard good things about you, so if you see something, give me a call tonight. But I don't want anyone to know." He said he wanted to call his trainer, Neil Drysdale, and tell him before he found out from someone else.

I told him I had this filly I liked a lot, and he said, "Okay, just let me know and get back to me." I hung up the phone and told J. B. I had a new guy, but I can't say who it is. He doesn't want me telling anyone. J. B. asked, "Well, what does that mean?" And I told him, "It means we can start looking again, boys, we're back in action."

We started looking at everything. And I'll tell you, we still had some bounce in our step after dragging our asses all over the place. I really liked this little Gulch filly, so I went over to Bob Lewis and asked him what he was going to do. He said Wayne was going to buy her for the Irish and he wasn't going to bid against them. One thing about Wayne, when he has all these guys with him, he tells them who's going to buy what, so they don't bid against each other. I told Bob I just wanted to know what he was going to do, because he knew I liked that filly. One thing I didn't want to do was bid against Bob.

When the filly came in the ring, I was out in the back, behind the pavilion, and I called Mr. Jones. She went up to around $600,000, then kept going steadily to $900,000. She went to $950,000 and I hit her at a million bucks. I'll never forget, I held my index finger up, signifying one...million...dollars. Then, just like that, the next bid goes to a million fifty. I told Mr. Jones what she was up to, and he said, "Well, are we in?"And I told him, "No, we're out right now." He said, "Well, hit her." I told him, "No, that's just too much for her. I'll find another one."

He said, "Okay, I'll talk to you tomorrow." As soon as he hung up, J. B. turned to me said, "I don't know who this new guy is, but I like him." Demi O'Byrne wound up buying the filly. She went to Europe, but I think she got hurt and never did much.

The next night, I had two colts that I liked — a Storm Cat and a Danzig. Mr. Jones had told me how he bought all these Danzigs and they got hurt. But this one was a big, good-looking, stout sonofagun who was being sold by John Mabee. I went back to look at the Storm Cat. He was a bit immature looking, but there was something about him I really liked. Plus, he had a very strong pedigree. I told Mr. Jones I was still between both colts, and I wanted to see what they looked like in the back of the ring. I wanted to see them when they were pumped up and how they reacted to the crowd. I never make up my mind until I see them back there. You never know if they're going to wash out or do something stupid.

It just so happened, the two colts were selling one after another, so I was able to see them at the same time. The Danzig colt walked with his head sort of high and I didn't like that. But the Storm Cat colt looked great, so I called Mr. Jones and told him that's who I was going for. He asked me what I thought he was going to bring, and I told him he was going to bring some heavy money. He just looked so good back here. I said he'd probably go for between eight hundred grand and a million. Mr. Jones said, in case he lost me on the cell phone, he didn't want to go over a million.

The more I looked at the horse, the more I loved him. Before he sold, I went to Bob Lewis, and he asked me if I was going to buy anything for him. I said I wasn't, because I had this colt at the Fasig-Tipton sale the next day I wanted to buy for him. That turned out to be Straight Man. I just wanted to let him know where I stood with him.

The Storm Cat colt went in the ring, and I called Mr. Jones on his car phone, because he was on his way to a doctor's or dentist's appointment. The bidding started at two hundred grand, but I never jump in until it starts to mellow out. It started to die off at $600,000 and I jumped in at $625,000. It went up to $650,000 and just then, I lost Mr. Jones on the phone. I tried to call him back and the phone was busy. He was trying to call me, and Mrs. Jones was telling him, "Don't try to call him back. He'll call you." I finally reached him, and he asked me what was going on. I told him it's still going and we're live at eight-fifty. When he went to $925,000, I knew I was nearing the end, so I put up the old index finger again at a million.

Just like that, it went to a $1,025,000. He had me hit him again at a $1,050,000, and it went to $1,075,000. I said, "Should I hit him again, Mr. Jones?" He asked me, "Do you like him?" I said, "Mr. Jones, I love him." And he told me, "Well, don't let him get away."

I hit him at $1,100,000. They came back at $1,150,000. I didn't know who I was up against, but I figured it had to be Lukas or Demi O'Byrne. It kept going back and forth in twenty-five and fifty thousand dollar jumps, and when I hit him at $1,200,000, they jumped it to $1,300,000 — a hundred thousand dollar jump. I countered with $1,400,000, just to let them know we were serious. They waited and waited, and finally went to $1,450,000. It took them a long time, and I told Mr. Jones, "We got them now. They're weakening." I immediately jumped back at $1,500,000 and that was it. He was ours.

When it was over, the word started spreading that I had bought the horse. There were these guys who were sitting behind Bob Lewis, and they told me that Lukas went, "Bob Baffert? Bob, he didn't buy him for you by mistake, did he?" Bob told him I never would have done that. I would have told him if I was buying a horse for him. Lukas asked where the hell I would have gotten $1,500,000, because he knew Mike Pegram would never go that high. Bob told him he had no idea what the deal was.

As soon as the hammer fell, I looked up and there was this swarm of photographers and reporters swinging around the corner and heading toward me. I signed the slip, 'Bob Baffert, agent.' I was on the phone with Mr. Jones and I said to him, "Oh my God, here comes the press. You ought to see the wave of reporters and photographers coming. What the hell did you get me into?"

I have to admit, I was really pumped up. That was a pretty good jolt of adrenaline. I couldn't believe how my hands were shaking while I was signing that slip. I kept thinking, "I hope that really was Aaron Jones I was talking to."

Buying the sales topper at Keeneland July like that was an awesome feeling. And I felt good about it, because I really liked this horse. As it turned out, I was bidding against Lukas and Bob Lewis. It actually was a partnership between Bob and Prince Ahmed bin Salman of The Thoroughbred Corp., up to a million dollars. Then the Prince backed out. Lukas had put the partnership together and had Demi O'Byrne back off on this horse. When Bob quit at

$1,450,000, Lukas was trying to make hand signals to Demi O'Byrne across the way that he was done, but it was too late.

One reporter who had been hanging around with us, said he had asked Lukas, "Isn't it ironic that you got outbid by Baffert, who was bidding against Bob Lewis just after winning the Kentucky Derby for him?" Wayne told him he thought it was really good for me, because I had four kids and this horse put some beans on the table for me. I told the reporter, "What's wrong with that? I like beans."

One thing I learned from Wayne is that these older guys are people who have already made their money and now they want to enjoy it and compete at the highest level. When you see a good one, you have to step up and buy that horse, because if one of them turns out, it pays for the rest and keeps them in the game, especially if they have the pedigree. You can't always count on going out there and finding these freaks of nature, so now I buy everything — the expensive ones and the freaks of nature — and hope one of them hits. If one or two do hit, then I'm still in the show.

Meanwhile, everybody wanted to know who the buyer was, and all I could tell them was that it was a new guy. He didn't want to divulge his identity, but he'd let everyone know the next day. When I got back to Del Mar, Mr. Jones told me he and Marie wanted to meet me and take me out to dinner. I took Bill with me and we were supposed to meet them at this restaurant in Rancho Santa Fe. I brought Bill because he was good with older people. I always had trouble with them. I like training for these elderly rich guys, but I'm not really big on socializing with them. I just can't get comfortable around them. I'm basically a kid at heart, and I like acting like a kid.

Bill asked me if I knew the guy, and I said I had never met him, but I had this picture of him I had cut out of the *Daily Racing Form.* They had run it with the story on the sale. So Bill and I went into the restaurant, and I'm looking at this picture of Mr. Jones, trying to recognize him. As soon as we got in, I saw this guy stand up at his table and wave his hands at me. I went over and showed him the picture I had and said, "Well, this looks like you."

We talked about everything, and he told me how he had gotten started. Bill hit it off with Marie and talked to her about wines and stuff like that. He asked her what they were going to call the horse. Marie loves the horses and enjoys getting involved in the whole scene. They really are a cute couple. She said, "I think I'm going to call him Seneca J." They've named several horses after their Seneca Sawmill. Bill, the kiss-ass that he is, said, "Oh, that's great. What a wonderful name." Mrs. Jones is really sharp and can read people pretty well. She said to me, "Bob, what do you think? You don't seem too excited about that name."

I told her, "I don't like it." The next thing I know, Bill is kicking me under the table. Mrs. Jones wanted to know why I didn't like it, and I said, "I just don't. I've got to live with the horse every day. And I can't picture myself saying, 'Let's bring Seneca J out.' You just spent a million and a half for the horse; he's got to have a better name than that. Why not think of a name that has to do with lumber, like Timber Cat or something."

The next day, I went to the track and met with Mr. and Mrs. Jones. It was funny, because Mrs. Jones went to introduce me to some friends, and said, "I'd like you to meet our new trainer, Bill Baffert."

She said to me, "I don't understand why you don't like Seneca J. It bothers me that you don't like it." I told her, every time you look at an Arabian horse, they always have an initial in their name, and to me it just didn't sound right. She said if I didn't feel right with it, they'd think of something else. They tried to put Timber Cat in, but it was taken, so they came up with Forestry. They asked me how I liked it, and I said I loved it.

When I got the horse, I told them he was immature, and if I tried to get him to the Kentucky Derby, I'd ruin him. I said he was a very good horse, but mentally and physically, he wasn't ready for it. And Mr. and Mrs. Jones were fine with that.

As it turned out, we also had Prime Timber, who won the San Felipe in 1999, then finished second in the Santa Anita Derby, and fourth in the Kentucky Derby, beaten only about two lengths. He really didn't kick in turning for home, and we found out after the race when we shod him that he had a little crack in the bar of his hoof. It grew out okay, but it had to be killing him in the race. As for Forestry, he has come around and turned into a top-class horse, winning several stakes, including the Dwyer. He's now worth almost eight times what I paid for him.

The purchase of Prime Timber was kind of amusing. The McKathan brothers found him at an Ocala two-year-olds in training sale. I didn't want to go down there, so J. B. sent me a video of some of the horses they liked. I loved this one Sultry Song colt, whose original name was Winewomenandsong. I told J. B. I wanted him and that I'd find a buyer right away. I had just picked up my twelve-year-old son Taylor from school and had him in the car with me. He really doesn't know what's going on with the races that much, but he's sharp. I called Mr. Jones and told him I really liked this Sultry Song colt. He worked in :21⅗ in a rainstorm and he was a strong, good-looking horse. Prime Timber reminded me a lot of Silver Charm the way he moved. I said these were the kind of horses we had to buy if we wanted to get to the Derby.

Mr. Jones said to buy him, so I called J. B. and told him, "Go ahead and vet him. We're going to buy him." After I hung up, Taylor said, "Hey dad, who's going to buy the horse?" I told him a new client I had named Aaron Jones. Taylor asked, "Why are you going to buy the horse for him?" I explained to him that I'm trying to get him a good horse, and he said, "Why don't you buy him for us? Don't buy him for him. He sounds like a good one." I guess I put on a good sales pitch. I even had my twelve-year-old convinced how good he was.

We bought Prime Timber for $375,000, and three months before the Derby, we turned down $6,000,000 for him. We didn't win the Derby, but for our first try, we made a pretty good run at it. And more importantly, I think Mr. and Mrs. Jones found the fun they were looking for.

LIVING IN NEVER LAND

"Bob has always wanted to succeed, but he certainly wasn't obsessed with it back when we first got married. He was always a super laid-back guy. He'd come home and play Nintendo for hours, and he had other interests. When he started to get into the Thoroughbreds, it was a humbling experience in the beginning. Here he was at the top of his profession with the Quarter Horses, and he wasn't winning many races with the Thoroughbreds. It wasn't until he came so close to winning the Derby with Cavonnier that be became obsessed with getting back there and succeeding. Now, it's seven days a week, and stress, and traveling all the time. He never takes a day off. I ask him, 'Are you happy? You've reached the top. You've achieved what you wanted. Has it made you happy?' "

— Sherry Baffert

Aaron Jones told me recently that he believed trainers should not be allowed to get married. You really do have to make a tremendous sacrifice. There are a lot of trainers out there who are happily married and have time to spend with their children, but most of them cannot compete at the level we're competing at.

To compete at that level and stay at the top, you cannot let up for a second. If I go a weekend without winning a stakes, I feel the barn is in a slump. My own mother told me after the 1999 Belmont Stakes, "Bob, you're in a slump."

Sherry used to be into the horses a little when we first started dating, but I really think I burned her out. If you marry someone who has as much passion for the sport as you do, it's one thing, but when it's not part of their life, it can make things difficult. I'm just very fortunate Sherry is such a wonderful mother and has done such a great job with the kids. I realize I'm missing a lot. This year, I missed out on my kids' baseball and basketball games and other events, and I feel horrible when they have to tell me all about it. But I've waited all my life to get to this level and I just can't let up. I feel like I have to be there for every work.

Sometimes, if I have a bad weekend, I think maybe it's my lifestyle. Maybe I'm doing something wrong. But then I'll win a big race, and it's like getting a high. It puts a bounce back in my step. I believe in karma, and sometimes I can feel it zing into me. Every win, regardless of how small, is like a drug.

Although I always wanted to be the best, I never dreamed of getting to where I am now. I was just some kid from Arizona who couldn't even put a halter or a vet wrap on a horse. To dream of attaining what I have would be like someone dreaming of becoming president. Every day, I give thanks for being so lucky. I've loved horses since I was a little boy, and I've gotten to work with them all my life. I want to remain that little boy forever. I don't ever want to grow old. That's why on FOX's 1999 Hollywood Gold Cup telecast I agreed to dress up as Austin Powers and do the whole deal, dancing around and going, "Yeah, baby." Their idea was, if somebody is flipping through the channels and all of a sudden they see this Austin Powers bit, they'll go, "What the hell is this?" And they'll stay tuned.

There are so many doors that have opened for me. I have to admit it's an intoxicating feeling for an ordinary guy like me to meet so many celebrities and to have people recognize me on a plane and ask for my autograph. To have Tom Brokaw come over to me in New

York City and tell me what a fan he is of mine is a difficult feeling to put into words.

Throughout my entire training career, one question has always gone through my head: I wonder if these other guys are so much better than me? When it came to certain big trainers, I'd always say, "Man, I wish I could be like that guy." And then, when you get to that level, you say to yourself, "I can't believe I ever thought he was that much better than me." I think we all go through that. To be successful, you can never think you're not as good as the next guy, no matter who he is. It makes you more competitive when you put yourself on a higher level, and the more competitive you are, the more successful you're going to be.

I'm trying to get this across to my kids. My son Taylor was playing all these different sports, but he wasn't excelling at any one of them. I remember telling Sherry that he should pick a sport and concentrate on that and try to become the best at it, because if he can't be the best at what he wants to do, he's not going to enjoy it; he's not going to get any better at it.

When I was a jockey, the best advice I ever got was from Bobby Adair, who was one of the greatest Quarter Horse riders who ever lived. I was at Rillito Downs, and Bobby asked me if I was going to come that summer to ride at Los Alamitos. I had done a little riding there. I told him I wasn't, because I just wasn't good enough to compete with those guys. He said to me, "Well, if you can't compete at that level, why do you want to be a jockey? Why would you be content to compete at these little bush tracks?" I thought about what he said and I realized he was right. The next day, I quit riding for good.

From that day on, I've never thought I couldn't be the best at what I did. There are lots of people who train at the lower-level tracks who are very good trainers. But they don't want to compete at the higher level. They're happy where they are. With Taylor, or any of my kids, if he has a bad game of basketball, I don't say, "You did good. You'll get him next time." I tell him, "Taylor, you really sucked. You know why? Because you thought you couldn't play with that kid. You didn't have confidence in yourself, and you thought that kid was better than you. He wasn't better than you. He just out-played you, because you gave up too easily. You work on your game and really practice hard, and I guarantee you you'll be able to get around that guy."

One time, Taylor met his hero, Ken Griffey Jr., and he asked him how he got so good, and Griffey told that he never used to be that good, but he practiced constantly. Hearing it from someone like that really woke Taylor up. Now, he's the MVP in his school. He works that same kid he was intimidated by around the court like he wasn't even there. Now, it's the other kid who's intimidated by him.

I've learned a lot from dealing with my kids, and I've carried that over to the horses, especially the two-year-olds. You teach them that competitiveness at the early training stages, and you can see it come through. The great ones you don't have to teach. Everything they do is natural. But it's the others, the immature ones, that you have to keep after.

I know that, because I was very immature. That's why I didn't go to college right out of high school. I just felt I wasn't mature enough to handle it. When I came back as a freshman and I was a year older, I could see the difference in my confidence level. I was a pretty shy kid growing up, and it wasn't until I found the level I could compete at that my confidence began to grow.

Once I got confidence in myself and my ability, and believed I was good at what I did, I made it a point not to let anybody know just how good. That's the way I've gone through life. If you act like you know everything, people won't feed you information and open up to you. And in order to be good at anything, you have to constantly be learning. I love pumping people for information, because there is so much to learn and absorb out there.

When I started winning all these big races and training titles, people began asking how I did it. It must be my help. It must be all this big money behind me. That's fine with me, because I never want to show my hand. Let them wonder and believe what they want.

The reason I act like a kid, and people don't take me seriously, is because I still am a kid. To me, I'm an eighteen-year-old in a 46-year-old's body. And when I'm around a young horse, that kid in me can relate to the kid in the horse. That's the only way you can get into these young horses' heads, and my strong point is buying and training young horses.

The only way I've learned over the years is by trial and error. I never worked for anyone in my life, so I had to experience everything firsthand. The only bad habits I have are my own. When I made a mistake, and I've made a lot of them, I just had to make sure I never made that mistake again. And believe me, I've done some of the most stupid things with horses imaginable, and I still do, but at least they're my stupid things. They're done as a result of trial and error and not as a result of anything I've been taught.

The people who work for me are only allowed to make my stupid errors. That's the whole key to a good assistant. I always tell them, "You learn my system and do it the way I do it. If you do it your way and I don't know it, then we cannot make an adjustment." And it only takes one little stupid thing to mess up a horse. But I'm just so fortunate to be surrounded by so many talented people. They're the reason I don't burn out.

Most of the time, I can't even explain why I do something or why I pick out a certain individual at the sale. Because of my background, everything I do is from gut instinct. When I was in 4-H as a kid, we would judge horses, steers, pigs, and sheep. Judging the pigs was tough, because to me they were all fat-looking things that looked all the same. We'd have these judging shows with thirty or forty kids, and we'd have to put all the animals in each category in order of how good they looked. Then we'd have to give reasons why you ranked them the way you did and what you liked in particular about each animal.

I wound up winning the whole contest based on the order I picked them, but my reasons were horrible. They said they couldn't award me the first prize because my reasons were no good. I said, "Why do I have to give reasons? The main thing is to pick them, right?" I would just look at them for a few seconds, and go, "This one, this one, this one, and this one. That's it." Even today, when I pick out yearlings, people can't understand why I can't give a reason why I like a particular horse. If they look athletic enough that they can run and they look like I'll be able to keep them sound, that's it.

I've been around horses since I was four and I have a lot of compassion for them. I don't have a dog or a cat. These horses are my pets, and especially with the good ones, you get very close to them. That's why, when I read derogatory things about Silver Charm it upset me, because it was like talking about my child. When we finally decided to retire him, I was kind of relieved, because you always worry about that one bad misstep, and if anything had happened to that horse, I don't know if I would have been able to handle it.

I have reached a point where I would like to enjoy the quality of life a little more, and spend more time with my kids. But right now, I have to maintain this level to be able to do that, so I'm in sort of a Catch-22 situation. Maybe, some day soon, I'll be able to take it a little slower. No matter how much success I have, I'm just a big old kid inside this white-haired body. Sometimes, I get to feeling sorry for myself when things aren't going well. But now I realize that life is too short to worry about things that aren't worth worrying about.

I used to look back, but now I just try to learn from my mistakes and keep on truckin'. This is the life people dream about having, and I have it. Regardless of what the future holds, it's been an incredible journey.

STAKES WINNERS

THOROUGHBRED
1982-PRESENT

QUARTER HORSE
1975-1991

STAKES WINNERS

YEAR	HORSE	OWNER	STAKES RACE
1982	March Speed	J. Peter Bogle	Turquoise Futurity

TOTALS FOR 1982: 32 starts, 9 wins, 1 stakes win, $10,986 in stable earnings

YEAR	HORSE	OWNER	STAKES RACE
1990	Broadway's Top Gun	Romi Stable	Ladbroke Futurity
		(Mike Pegram & Bob Roth)	Phoenix Futurity
	Frosty Freeze	Romi Stable	Watch Wendy Stakes
			Reasonable Force Handicap
	Theresa's Pleasure	Lester Smith	Proud Sister Stakes
			California Thoroughbred Breeders' Association Stakes
			California Cup Juvenile Fillies Stakes

TOTALS FOR 1990: 143 starts, 36 wins, 7 stakes wins, $882,042 in stable earnings

YEAR	HORSE	OWNER	STAKES RACE
1991	Broadway's Top Gun	Romi Stable	Bolsa Chica Stakes
	Charmonnier	Robert H. Walter	Wells Fargo Bank California Cup Classic Handicap
	Ebonair	Robert B. & Beverly J. Lewis	California Cup Juvenile Stakes
	Gundaghia	John Goodman	Governor's Cup Handicap
		& Robert Kieckhefer	Hollywood Turf Express Handicap
	Letthebighossroll	Romi Stable	Zany Tactics Stakes
			Piedmont Stakes

YEAR	HORSE	OWNER	STAKES RACE
			Harry Henson Stakes
			El Cajon Stakes
			California Cup Sprint Handicap
	Soviet Sojourn	Hal J. Earnhardt	Junior Miss Stakes
			Sorrento Stakes

TOTALS FOR 1991: 139 starts, 33 wins, 12 stakes wins, $1,447,362 in stable earnings

YEAR	HORSE	OWNER	STAKES RACE
1992	Arches of Gold	Mike Pegram & Bob Roth	La Brea Stakes
	Boss Soss	Robert B. & Beverly J. Lewis	San Mateo Juvenile Stakes
	Gundaghia	John Goodman	Aprisa Handicap
		& Robert Kieckhefer	Governor's Cup
			Vernon O. Underwood Stakes
	No Mecourtney	Robert B. & Beverly J. Lewis	Novel Sprite Handicap
	Thirty Slews	De Groot, Dutch Masters III	Bing Crosby Handicap
		& Pegram	CERF Sprint Handicap
			Breeders' Cup Sprint
	Wheeler Oil	Mike Pegram	De Anza Stakes

TOTALS FOR 1992: 192 starts, 39 wins, 10 stakes wins, $1,687,354 in stable earnings

YEAR	HORSE	OWNER	STAKES RACE
1993	Arches of Gold	Mike Pegram & Bob Roth	Camilla Urso Handicap
			Cascapedia Handicap
	Flagship Commander	Robert Kieckhefer	Ladbroke Futurity
	Gundaghia	John Goodman	Crazy Kid Handicap
		& Robert Kieckhefer	Aprisa Handicap

189

YEAR	HORSE	OWNER	STAKES RACE
	Miss Gibson County	Mike Pegram	Moraga Futurity
			Phoenix Futurity

TOTALS FOR 1993: 214 starts, 42 wins, 7 stakes wins, $1,353,892 in stable earnings

YEAR	HORSE	OWNER	STAKES RACE
1994	Arches of Gold	Mike Pegram & Bob Roth	Jandy Stud Farm Handicap
			Dahlia Stakes
	Charlies Paradise	Mike Pegram	Moraga Stakes
			Dominant Dancer Stakes
			Bustles and Bows Stakes
			Phoenix Futurity
	Gundaghia	John Goodman	El Conejo Handicap
		& Robert Kieckhefer	Montclair Handicap
			Aprisa Handicap
	Letthebighossroll	Mike Pegram & Bob Roth	George Warwick Handicap
	Miss Gibson County	Mike Pegram	Prima Donna Stakes
	Sir Hutch	Robert B. & Beverly J. Lewis	Potrero Grande Handicap
	Viva El Capitan	Maynard Davis	Jungle Savage Stakes
		& Charles Novak	

TOTALS FOR 1994: 249 starts, 49 wins, 13 stakes wins, $1,944,341 in stable earnings

YEAR	HORSE	OWNER	STAKES RACE
1995	Argolid	Mike Pegram	On Trust Handicap
	Argonnier	Mr. & Mrs. Robert H. Walter	I'm Smokin Stakes
	Batroyale	Mr. & Mrs. Robert H. Walter	Sorrento Stakes
			Del Mar Debutante Stakes

YEAR	HORSE	OWNER	STAKES RACE
	Boulderdash Bay	Robert A. Canning	Woody Erin Handicap
	Cavonnier	Mr. & Mrs. Robert H. Walter	California Stallion Stakes
			Budweiser California Cup Juvenile
	Gundaghia	John Goodman	Governor's Cup Handicap
		& Robert Kieckhefer	Bull Dog Stakes
	Let's Be Curious	Plato & Wistaria Racing Stables	San Jacinto Handicap
	Letthebighossroll	Mike Pegram	Crazy Kid Stakes

TOTALS FOR 1995: 363 starts, 79 wins, 11 stakes wins, $2,590,253 in stable earnings

YEAR	HORSE	OWNER	STAKES RACE
1996	Argonnier	Walter Family Trust	Zany Tactics Stakes
			Real Good Deal Stakes
	Boulderdash Bay	Robert A. Canning	Cardmania Stakes
	Cavonnier	Walter Family Trust	El Camino Real Derby
			Santa Anita Derby
	Criollito (ARG)	Robert B. & Beverly J. Lewis	Churchill Downs Handicap
	In Excessive Bull	Hal J. Earnhardt	Hollywood Prevue Stakes
			California Breeders' Champion
			Stakes
	Isitingood	Terry Henn & Mike Pegram	Longacres Mile Handicap
			Fayette Stakes
			Clark Handicap
	Letthebighossroll	Mike Pegram	Triple Bend Breeders' Cup Handicap
			Answer Do Stakes
			Crazy Kid Handicap
	Semoran	Donald R. Dizney	Foster City Stakes
		& James E. English	Remington Park Derby

191

YEAR	HORSE	OWNER	STAKES RACE
	Silver Charm	Robert B. & Beverly J. Lewis	Del Mar Futurity
	The Texas Tunnel	Mike Pegram	Beau Brummel Stakes
			Broadway's Top Gun Stakes

TOTALS FOR 1996: 340 starts, 77 wins, 19 stakes wins, $4,468,929 in stable earnings

YEAR	HORSE	OWNER	STAKES RACE
1997	Anet	Double Diamond Farm	Rushaway Stakes
		& Donald R. Dizney	USA Stakes
			Del Mar Derby
			Lone Star Derby
	Batoile	Walter Family Trust	Real Good Deal Stakes
	Batroyale	Walter Family Trust	Bay Meadows Matron Handicap
	Best Star	Golden Eagle Farm	El Cajon Stakes
	Commitisize	Mike Pegram	Hollywood Prevue Stakes
	Ex Marks the Cop	Maynard Davis	California Sires Stakes
		& Charles R. Novak	California Cup Juvenile Stakes
	Fiscal Year	Golden Eagle Farm	Generous Portion Stakes
	Fun in Excess	Mike Pegram	California Cup Matron Handicap
	High Stakes Player	Mike Pegram	El Conejo Handicap
			Palos Verdes Handicap
			Count Fleet Sprint Handicap
			Aristides Handicap
	Holy Nola	Mike Pegram	Great Arizona Futurity Shoot-Out
	Inexcessive Speed	Mike Pegram	California Sires Stakes
	Isitingood	Terry Henn & Mike Pegram	The Bart Stakes
			New Orleans Handicap

YEAR	HORSE	OWNER	STAKES RACE
			Texas Mile Stakes
	Queen of Money	Mike Pegram	Santa Ynez Stakes
	Real Quiet	Mike Pegram	Hollywood Futurity
	Semoran	Donald R. Dizney	Prairie Meadows Cornhusker Handicap
			Kentucky Cup Classic Handicap
	Silver Charm	Robert B. & Beverly J. Lewis	San Vicente Stakes
			Kentucky Derby
			Preakness Stakes
	Souvenir Copy	Golden Eagle Farm	Del Mar Futurity
			Norfolk Stakes
	The Texas Tunnel	Mike Pegram	Foothill Stakes
	Vivid Angel	Ed & Natalie Friendly	Del Mar Debutante Stakes
			Oak Leaf Stakes

TOTALS FOR 1997: 430 starts, 113 wins, 33 stakes wins, $8,867,128 in stable earnings

YEAR	HORSE	OWNER	STAKES RACE
1998	Cavonnier	Walter Family Trust	Ack Ack Stakes
	Censored	Mike Pegram	Melair Stakes
	Commitisize	Mike Pegram	La Puente Stakes
			Cinema Handicap
			USA Stakes
	Excellent Meeting	Golden Eagle Farm	Del Mar Debutante Stakes
			Oak Leaf Stakes
			Hollywood Starlet Stakes
	Exploit	Robert B. & Beverly J. Lewis	Iroquois Stakes
			Brown & Williamson Kentucky

YEAR	HORSE	OWNER	STAKES RACE
			Jockey Club Stakes
	Fun in Excess	Mike Pegram	Run For the Roses Handicap
			Pro or Con Handicap
	High Stakes Player	Mike Pegram	Don Bernhardt Stakes
			Governor's Handicap
	Hookedonthefeelin	Mike Pegram	Landaluce Stakes
	Indian Charlie	Hal J. Earnhardt	Santa Anita Derby
		& John R. Gaines Racing Stable	
	Joe Who (BRZ)	James E. Helzer	Wickerr Handicap
			Live Dream Handicap
	Magical Allure	Golden Eagle Farm	CERF Stakes
			Torrey Pines Stakes
			Lady's Secret Breeders' Cup Handicap
			La Brea Stakes
			Fleet Treat Stakes
	Musical Sweep	Myron Sammons	Barretts Juvenile Stakes
	Premier Property	Hal J. Earnhardt	Sunny Slope Stakes
			Hollywood Prevue Stakes
	Real Quiet	Mike Pegram	Kentucky Derby
			Preakness Stakes
	Shot of Gold	Matt Young, et al	Rushaway Stakes
	Silver Charm	Robert B. & Beverly J. Lewis	San Fernando Breeders' Cup Stakes
			Strub Stakes
			Kentucky Cup Classic Handicap
			Goodwood Breeders' Cup Handicap
			Clark Handicap
			Dubai World Cup
	Silverbulletday	Mike Pegram	Debutante Stakes

YEAR	HORSE	OWNER	STAKES RACE
			Sorrento Stakes
			Walmac International Alcibiades Stakes
			Breeders' Cup Juvenile Fillies
			Golden Rod Stakes
	Souvenir Copy	Golden Eagle Farm	Derby Trial Stakes
	Stalwart Tsu	Coastal Concepts	Harry F. Brubaker Stakes
	Worldly Manner	Golden Eagle Farm	Best Pal Stakes
			Del Mar Futurity

TOTALS FOR 1998: 538 starts, 139 wins, 44 stakes wins, $15,000,870 in stable earnings

YEAR	HORSE	OWNER	STAKES RACE
1999	American Spirit	Donald R. Dizney	Baldwin Stakes
	Censored	Mike Pegram	Pro Or Con Handicap
			B. Thoughtful Stakes
	Chilukki	Stonerside Stable	Kentucky Breeders' Cup Stakes
			Debutante Stakes
	Classic Cat	Gary M. Garber	Tokyo City Handicap
			San Bernardino Handicap
	Commitisize	Mike Pegram	El Rincon Handicap
	Del Mar Gray	Ed & Natalie Friendly	Khaled Stakes
	Excellent Meeting	Golden Eagle Farm	Las Virgenes Stakes
			Santa Anita Oaks
			Fantasy Stakes
			Princess Stakes
	Exploit	Robert B. & Beverly J. Lewis	San Vicente Stakes
	Forestry	Aaron U. & Marie D. Jones	San Pedro Stakes
			Dwyer Stakes

YEAR	HORSE	OWNER	STAKES RACE
	General Challenge	Golden Eagle Farm	California Breeders' Champion Stakes
			Santa Catalina Stakes
			Santa Anita Derby
			Affirmed Handicap
	Hookedonthefeelin	Mike Pegram	Miss Preakness Stakes
	Joe Who (BRZ)	James E. Helzer	Firecracker Breeders' Cup Handicap
	Prime Timber	Aaron U. & Marie D. Jones	San Felipe Stakes
	Real Quiet	Mike Pegram	Pimlico Special Handicap
			Hollywood Gold Cup
	River Keen (IRE)	Hugo Reynolds	Bel Air Handicap
	Silver Charm	Robert B. & Beverly J. Lewis	San Pasqual Handicap
	Silverbulletday	Mike Pegram	Davona Dale Stakes
			Fair Grounds Oaks
			Ashland Stakes
			Kentucky Oaks
			Black-Eyed Susan Stakes
			Monmouth Breeders' Cup Oaks

TOTALS FOR 1999: 345 starts, 85 wins, 33 stakes wins, $8,201,217 in stable earnings*

*** through July 22, 1999**

STAKES WINNERS*

Gold Coast Express   1986 world champion

1986 champion three-year-old

1986 champion three-year-old gelding

1987 champion aged horse and champion aged gelding

Easygo Effort   1987 champion two-year-old gelding

Shawnes Favorite   1987 champion three-year-old

1987 champion three-year-old gelding

Ed Grimley   1991 champion two-year-old gelding

YEAR	HORSE	OWNER	STAKES RACE
1981	Kellys Coffer	Dorothy Boothe	Arizona Quarter Racing Association Lassie Stakes
			Prescott Downs Futurity
			Gila County Futurity
	Kellys Coffer	Myron Sammons	Santa Cruz County Futurity
	Twin Profit	Leo Hokama	Prescott Downs Derby
1982	Love N Money	Rulon Goodman	West Texas Derby
			Rillito Spring Derby
1985	Kellys Coffer	Dorothy Boothe	Alameda Handicap

YEAR	HORSE	OWNER	STAKES RACE
1986	Gold Coast Express	William and Louella Mitchell	Champion of Champions
			Dash For Cash Derby
			Sophomore Handicap
			Laddie Handicap
1987	Doctor Ro	Roi W. Young	Ed Burke Memorial Futurity
			Pilgrim Handicap
	Easygo Effort	Schuck & Sons	Golden State Futurity
	Gold Coast Express	William and Louella Mitchell	Vessels Maturity
			Los Alamitos Invitational
			Championship
			Clabbertown G Handicap
	Hollies Effort	Holly Golightly	Santa Cruz County Futurity
			Las Ninas Handicap
	Knights Wheeler	Hal Earnhardt	Josie's Bar Handicap
			Lassie Handicap
			Foster City Handicap
	Zure Hope Again	Dutch Masters III	PCQHRA Breeders' Futurity
1988	Doctor Ro	Roi W. Young	Josie's Bar Handicap
	Easygo Effort	Schuck & Sons	Laddie Handicap
			PCQHRA Breeders' Derby
			Dash For Cash Derby
	Elite Empress	Willard and Greg Ballenger	Jet Deck Handicap
			Pacific Handicap
	Sail On Hawaii	Steve Winegardner	PCQHRA Breeders' Futurity

YEAR	HORSE	OWNER	STAKES RACE
	Gold Coast Express	William and Louella Mitchell	Peninsula Championship
			Clabbertown G Handicap
	Shawnes Favorite	Salinas Ranch	Champion of Champions
			Los Alamitos Invitational
			Championship
			Pomona Invitational Handicap
	Zip Into Cash	Dutch Masters III	California Sires Cup Futurity
			Bardella Handicap
	Zure Hope Again	Dutch Masters III	Los Alamitos Derby
			QHBC Pacific Classics Derby
			Gold Coast Express Invitational
1989	Collectors Series	David Davenport	California Sires Cup Derby
	Elite Empress	Willard and Greg Ballenger	Vandy's Flash Handicap
			(finished in a dead-heat)
			Lassie Handicap
	Ourautograph	San Tan Tillage Inc.	Kindergarten Futurity
	Streakin Jewel	Harvey Pickens	PCQHRA Breeders' Futurity
	Zure Hope Again	Dutch Masters III	Go Man Go Handicap
1990	Genuine Article	Kim A. Kessinger	Gold Rush 870 Derby
	Miss Strikin Jet	San Tan Tillage Inc.	Kevin Burns Memorial Futurity
			Leo Handicap
	Ourautograph	San Tan Tillage Inc.	Sophomore Handicap
			Laddie Handicap
			Vandy's Flash Handicap

YEAR	HORSE	OWNER	STAKES RACE
			St. Nicholas Express Handicap
			Garden Grove Handicap
1991	Ed Grimley	Mitch DeGroot	Bay Meadows Futurity
	Miss Strikin Jet	Hal and Karen Phenix	Debutante Handicap
	Rush Fora First Down	Robert H. Kieckhefer	California Sires Cup Futurity
			QHBC Freshman Classic
	Shake Six	Stripsky Enterprises	Calyx Invitational Handicap
			San Jose Handicap
			Hillsdale Handicap

B A F F E R T ' S

QUARTER HORSE RECORD

YEAR	STARTS	WINS	EARNINGS
1975	12	0	$372
1977	46	6	$24,573
1978	7	3	$995
1979	55	21	$29,247
1980	39	18	$55,691
1981	237	87	$210,179
1982	262	73´	$247,318
1983	179	49	$120,924
1984	179	33	$123,824
1985	269	52	$239,889
1986	484	122	$697,927
1987	633	156	$1,468,009
1988	717	148	$1,713,759
1989	523	96	$1,057,860
1990	448	83	$764,950
1991	159	31	$489,498
Lifetime	**4,249**	**978**	**$7,245,015**

* Information provided by the American Quarter Horse Association

INDEX

PHOTO CREDITS

Family photographs *(courtesy of the Baffert family)*; weighing in *(Milt Martinez)*; Gold Coast Express *(Ty Wyantt)*; Thirty Slews *(Barbara D. Livingston)*; Breeders' Cup winner's circle *(Skip Dickstein)*; with Mike Pegram *(Skip Dickstein)*; 1996 Derby finish line *(Churchill Downs)*; with the Monsignor *(Anne M. Eberhardt)*; with Cavonnier at Pimlico *(Barbara D. Livingston)*; at Pimlico *(Barbara D. Livingston)*;

Silver Charm winning Del Mar Futurity *(Benoit & Associates)*; with Silver Charm at Churchill Downs *(Skip Dickstein)*; Silver Charm winning 1997 Kentucky Derby *(Skip Dickstein)*; Baffert and media *(Barbara D. Livingston)*; with Silver Charm at Pimlico *(Barbara D. Livingston)*; in Pimlico winner's circle *(Skip Dickstein)*; Belmont Stakes crowd *(Barbara D. Livingston)*; on the way to the Belmont paddock *(Anne M. Eberhardt)*; with daughter Savannah *(Skip Dickstein)*; Dubai World Cup and trophy presentation *(Trevor Jones)*; Silver Charm and Baffert in Arab attire *(Tony Leonard)*;

"The Walk" — Derby 1998 *(Skip Dickstein)*; Derby rose *(Anne M. Eberhardt)*; with Kentucky Derby trophy *(Skip Dickstein)*; winner's circle *(Rick Samuels)*; with Kent Desormeaux at Pimlico *(Rick Samuels)*; Victory Gallop beating Real Quiet in 1998 Belmont Stakes *(Barbara D. Livingston)*; with wife Sherry and daughter Savannah at the Belmont Stakes *(Anne M. Eberhardt)*;

Baffert, D. Wayne Lukas, and Nick Zito *(Anne M. Eberhardt)*; with Bo Derek *(Anne M. Eberhardt)*; with Sonny Hine *(Skip Dickstein)*; with the Lewises *(Anne M. Eberhardt)*; with his cell phone *(Anne M. Eberhardt)*; as Austin Powers *(FOX)*; with Joe Torre *(The Blood-Horse)*; with Ken Griffey Jr. *(Benoit & Associates)*; with Sheikh Mohammed *(Anne M. Eberhardt)*; with Eclipse Award *(The Blood-Horse)*; Baffert and Silverbulletday *(Matt Goins)*.

Also from
The Blood-Horse, Inc.

Matriarchs: Great Mares of the 20th Century

Country Life Diary (revised edition)

Kentucky Derby Glasses Price Guide

Four Seasons of Racing

Cigar: America's Horse

Crown Jewels of Thoroughbred Racing

Whittingham

Royal Blood

Thoroughbred Champions: Top 100 Racehorses of the 20th Century

ABOUT THE AUTHORS

BOB BAFFERT is an Eclipse Award-winning trainer who counts Kentucky Derby winners Silver Charm and Real Quiet among his champions. A former Quarter Horse trainer, Baffert switched to Thoroughbreds in the early 1990s and had almost immediate success. His shock of white hair, humor, and horsemanship have made him the most recognizable figure in horse racing today. He is based in Southern California and trains for some of racing's most prominent owners.

Baffert (left), Pegram (center), and Haskin

STEVE HASKIN is an award-winning Turf writer and national correspondent for *The Blood-Horse*, the leading Thoroughbred industry weekly. Haskin spent twenty-nine years with *Daily Racing Form*, and became known for his insightful coverage of the Triple Crown races. Haskin won the Red Smith Award for best Kentucky Derby advance and the David Woods Award for best Preakness story in 1997.

Haskin has written for many publications, including *Thoroughbred Record*, *The Backstretch*, *Pacemaker International*, *The British Racehorse*, *Louisiana Horse*, *Stud & Stable*, and *The Sporting Chronicle*. He also has provided research for many book projects as well as to ABC-TV. He lives in Hamilton Square, New Jersey, with his wife and daughter.